"Matt has a gift to inspire others. This book is an absolute favorite of mine. Awesome work Matt!" -*Amazon Customer*

—◦∞◦—

"Uplifting, inspiring, and encouraging. Matt speaks to people as everyday folk. Easily relatable." -*Amazon Customer*

—◦∞◦—

"This book is a gift from God Himself. Matt's story is just the testimony I needed!" -*Amazon Customer*

—◦∞◦—

"Matt McMillen is authentic and gets to the point. God is using him to encourage and help many people come to Christ and enjoy their relationship with Him." -*Amazon Customer*

—◦∞◦—

"This book was absolutely amazing. Matt's ability to tell his personal story, and share the love of Christ was phenomenal. I loved the unconventional approach, it brought a level of sincerity that really shines through. Highly recommended." -*Amazon Customer*

Robert,
Jesus loves you unconditionally!
— Matt
1 John 3:1

Matt McMillen is a bestselling Christian author and teacher of God's Word. His books and massive social media ministry has taught countless amounts of people their true identity in Christ. Matt's easy-to-understand biblical teachings have helped build confidence in his readers, break life-long addictions, and find their true purpose for living: enjoying God's grace through Jesus Christ!

For more information on his ministry, visit:
www.mattmcmillenministries.com

TRUE PURPOSE
IN JESUS CHRIST

TRUE PURPOSE IN JESUS CHRIST

Finding the Relationship for Which You Were Made

MATT MCMILLEN

www.MattMcMillenMinistries.com

True Purpose in Jesus Christ
by
Matt McMillen
Email: matt@mattmcmillen.com

Copyright© 2016 by Matt McMillen
Revised 2017

Matt McMillen Ministries, L.L.C.
720 West Karsch Blvd.
Farmington, Missouri 63640

Ordering Information:

Quantity sales. Special discounts are available on quantity purchases by corporations, associations, U.S. trade bookstores, wholesalers, and others. For details contact the publisher at the address above.

Publisher's Cataloging-in-Publication data
McMillen, Matt
True Purpose in Jesus Christ/Matt McMillen
ISBN: 099715330X
ISBN 9780997153309
Religion

First Edition

14 13 12 11 10 / 10 9 8 7 6 5 4 3 2 1

For Grandma. Thank you for showing me who Jesus really is.

CONTENTS

Delight yourself in the Lord,
and He will give you the desires of your heart.

PSALM 37:4

PREFACE

Hello there! Thank you for picking up this book! By you doing so, you are helping me fulfill my purpose for living. Before I begin, I have to tell you that everything in this book is based on actually *knowing* Jesus Christ as your personal Savior. So, before I tear into all of this "Jesus talk," I want to invite *you* to join *me* in a relationship with *Him*! No, you don't *have to* do this, to be able to read this book, but it will make a lot more sense if you do! Also, by you choosing (yes, this is your choice, nobody can ever force you to do this) to begin a relationship with Jesus, you will be joining hands with the Creator of the universe—and *that* is amazing.

Repeat this prayer with me, and you will instantly know Him and become a Christian:

> *"Hello Jesus. I know you already know my name and I know you already know who I am, but now I want to get to know who you are as well. Would you please help me do this? Yes, I am a sinner, I've made many mistakes in my life—I'm admitting that to you. Right now, I am asking you to forgive me of all of my sins and to remove all of my past mistakes. I believe you can do this, and I believe that ONLY you can do this! Change my life*

into what YOU want it to be! Thank you for this free gift of forgiveness! I'm all yours! Now, teach me how to love you, like you love me."

Friend, if you just said that prayer and you believed it as the truth, then welcome to the Family of God! From here on out *everything* changes for the better, forever! Now it's time to get to know Jesus more and more every day. I will help you with that, even if it's just a little.

Introduction

GOD LIKES YOU, A LOT

"I knew you before I formed you in your mother's womb"
-God

See JEREMIAH 1:5

"WHY AM I ALIVE?"

Your life is not random. Absolutely nothing about you is random. From your looks, to your style, to your personality—to your likes and dislikes—God wanted you to be *you*. He also wanted you to be specifically placed on this planet at this exact time in order to make an impact on *this* particular generation, and He did all of this with great planning! God knew about you *before* He created Adam and Eve, He even knew your name! (See Jeremiah 1:5, Hebrews 11:3). That's how important you are to Him! Your exact DNA structure was pre-planned by God *on* purpose, and *for* a wonderful purpose—an eternal purpose! (See John 14:3).

Why did He do all of this planning *just* for you to be alive? Because He loves you! Out of everything He's created, from the sun, the moon, all of the stars, to planet earth and every creature that dwells on it, *you* as one of His beloved children, are God's most favorite creation. You are part of mankind, a people created in His image. You resemble God! And you exist because of His deep love for you! It's really that simple.

God specifically engineered everything about this planet to give you life. From gravity, to oxygen, to the ozone—if it's part of the geological make-up of the universe, then it was intelligently designed by God so that us human beings can live. Even the exact distance we are from the sun—which is not too close that we burn up, yet not too far away that we freeze—God engineered that distance *perfectly*. We humans are why there is *something* rather than *nothing*. We are also the *why* everything is so beautiful and in order. God shaped all of this *exclusively* so we can have life! He created all of this raw material for us! Our Creator has even tilted this planet at *just* the right axis, and He is causing it to spin at *just* the right speed, at *just* the right distance from the moon, stars, and every other planet—for us! Our lives *are* God's glory! We are His idea! Which proves this:

> All of Creation exists so that we would be able to *have* life, *sustain* life, and *enjoy* life.

You, _____ (insert full name here), are so dearly loved by God that He planned for your life to happen even before He laid down the foundation of this vast universe. You are meticulously, intentionally, and *lovingly* engineered by God's own hands for a wonderful purpose. YOU BEING ALIVE IS NOT ACCIDENTAL.

You were created *by* someone, and *for* someone, and that *Someone* is God Almighty, the God of the Bible. You might *think* that you came from your parents, but your parents had no clue who you would be—God however, did. With all due respect to them, your parents were simply the vessels which carried you, God is the one who actually *made* you. You are the imagination of God, brought to life! He was excited and joyful about creating you! That in itself should make you feel absolutely amazing! God loved you *so* much that He hand-crafted you! He didn't *have* to make you, but He chose to, out of love.

Which brings me to my next point: *Love*. Ultimately, the universe was formed and you were created to have a loving relationship with God—forever—*beginning* in these temporary bodies, and then continuing on into eternity. "How do I get in on this love from God?" you might ask. The answer to that question is extremely simple, and it was *made* simple by God. Also, the *answer* is the entire reason why I wrote this book. If you boiled it down to its purest form, in order to have uninterrupted access to a loving relationship with our Creator, He requires you to do one thing: *Place your faith in His one and only begotten Son, Jesus Christ.*

Does that sound too easy? That's because it is! The devil wants you to think this isn't true because it's way too easy, *or* that you need to add more to it. He wants you to think it's extremely difficult to become a Christian, and he also wants you to think that you have to keep earning God's love after you get it for the very first time through Christ. That's wrong too.

God loved you *before* time began. You didn't earn His love in the first place, it was handed to you. All *we* do is simply accept it undeservedly by grace through our faith in Jesus' forgiveness (see Ephesians 2:8-9). You could look at it this way: *Jesus paid off a debt with the Father that we would never be able to pay for on our own. We now have a connection to this sin debt pay off through our belief and acceptance of Christ's deity.* I'll go deep into this subject along with repentance and other biblical matters in much greater detail, later.

However, when you finally understand that you don't have to keep earning God's love through religious works—and that you can't *lose* God's love through bad attitudes and behaviors—you finally come to a place of peace and a rest unlike you've ever known before (see Hebrews 4:11). When you get to this point in your relationship with God you understand *grace*. God is full of grace (see Titus 2:11, Ephesians 1:6, Romans 3:24). Grace is what makes Him different than all of the other fake gods—none offer it but Him. Grace is loving, *undeserved* kindness and favor.

But first you have to personally accept God's grace through Christ's free gift (see Romans 10:13, 2 Corinthians 5:20). How? By believing it and then receiving it! You simply say or think, "Yes, I believe it and I receive it." After that it's y yours! Absolutely *nothing* and absolutely *nobody* can ever take it away!

You might be thinking, "I really like that. I really *want* that, but I don't know if I can actually *receive* this loving gift. I've done way too many bad things in my life to be acceptable to God. Plus, I don't know enough of the Bible." To that I would say, "So what! That's not important!" My friend, God isn't concerned about those things. As for your past, He actually wants to use it for your future (see Revelation 12:11). Don't be intimidated by the Bible, it is simply a compilation of love letters from your Heavenly Dad. Those letters are meant to encourage you and teach you, not make you feel bad or obligated to memorize them.

God is simply looking for your effort and willingness to place your faith in Christ. He wants you to begin to show Jesus love and respect with your words and actions while simply being yourself. After that, everything else falls right into place despite your past or knowledge of Scripture. There are no prerequisites to becoming a Christian, not one. Do you believe in and accept Jesus Christ's forgiveness? Yes? Then you're good! Stop worrying about whether or not you're saved, and instead begin to *grow* in your relationship with Him! God takes it from there!

Maybe you *still* can't get this into your heart—your head won't let you. Here is a short little lesson that really helped me understand how we *get* Jesus:

Let's say someone walked up to you and asked for a dollar to get something to eat. You reply, "Sure," then hand a dollar out to them—but they don't *take* the dollar from your hand, it just hangs there, dangling. However, they say it again, "Can I have a dollar?" Confused, because you are handing them a dollar to take, you say it again, "Yes. Here, take this dollar. It's free. You don't even have to pay me back." But they say it *again*, "Can I *please* have a dollar?! I *really* need a dollar from you desperately!" Finally, your reply is, "Yes, you can have this dollar, take it, it's right here. I'm handing it to you but you have to take it out of my hand and receive it."

So many unbelievers ask God for a "dollar" all the time, but still refuse to believe in Christ alone. He too, is standing right in front of them, willing and ready to give Himself away. His palms are held open, arms stretched out, and He is smiling warmly. Yet, so many people never receive what God wants us to take from Him. Friend, *receive* Him, today.

Another one of the devil's tactics is he wants you to think you are being naive or foolish when you place your faith in Jesus Christ. *Doubt* is one of Satan's greatest weapons—he will kill you with it if you're not careful! (See James 1:6, Acts 14:2, 2 Thessalonians 2:12). He started this deception with Eve in the Garden of Eden and it continues on with us. One of the keys to overcoming doubt is to study the life of Christ. As a Christian, Jesus lives in you, so read about Him.

One of my main goals for writing this book is to help teach you about Satan's tricks. Once you begin to recognize him and his evil schemes, *then* you can kick him where it hurts! I'll teach you how to do this! But honestly, by you simply enjoying a close relationship with Jesus the enemy stands no chance against you. He's a little maggot. By allowing Jesus to live through you, you can have a strong, confident faith, rather than a weak, constantly defeated, victim-style faith.

When dealing with Satan and his demons you can't physically grab them or slap them—although that'd be nice—but the way you *can* fight the devil and really leave him perplexed is by doing good things, by continually praising God, and by trusting Him *even* (and especially) when bad things or unfair situations are happening in your life. I want to teach you how to fight back! You fight back with love, joy, peace, patience, kindness, gentleness, and self-control! I want to build you *up* and instill in your soul just how much *power* lies deep within you because of your reborn spirit and Jesus Christ! (See Romans 6:6, Luke 10:19).

One of the main things I want to establish is when those unfair situations arise in your life—and they will—Jesus doesn't want you to fall apart. Instead, He wants you to keep your confidence in Him and He wants you to *continue* to trust Him. How? By showing Him love and respect with your words and actions—and by letting Him live *through* you. Try to remember that He's going to *use* your unfair situations for a good future purpose *if* you let Him! Jesus wants you to make choices based on what *He* would approve of—His Spirit lives in you so you *do* have this ability. Because of that, we do such things as forgive others like He has forgiven us. We even go so far as *blessing* those who do us wrong. Yes, bless them!

I'm not saying you have accept unacceptable behavior as normal—no way! As a matter of fact, Jesus wants you to do just the opposite. Don't *accept* it, but *handle* it how His Spirit leads you. This will require tons of loving sacrifice on your part, but as your relationship with Jesus grows, He will teach you how to do this by transforming your mindset.

When you've established biblical healthy boundaries with others, you will begin to treat even your worst enemies with kindness and a good attitude. The secret formula to enjoying the abundant life which Jesus came to give you is to trust Him enough to *not* choose to sin *even* when we are tremendously tempted to. Instead, we find our satisfaction in pleasing God and living *out* our true spiritual perfection (see Colossians 1:22, Philippians 2:12).

The Holy Spirit teaches us that when the enemy *tempts* us to go against our holy character, we pause, then replace that incorrect thought with a truthful thought—one that matches up with who we are in spirit: *children of God* (see John 1:12, Galatians 3:26, Philippians 4:8, Galatians 2:20, 2 Corinthians 5:17). This is extremely difficult to do at first, because of our old stinking thinking and the flesh—which has led us for so long—but it gets easier as you go deeper into your relationship with Jesus. Eventually, you *enjoy* living out your life as God's own child!

Another way you will be able to defeat the devil's power in your life is by refusing to have a pity-party—ever. Self-pity ruined my life for years, and I never even recognized it as coming from the pits of hell until I got to know Jesus better. As new creations in Christ, we should never feel sorry for ourselves because by doing so we are opening up opportunities for the enemy to go to work.

I'm not saying you should ignore your feelings, in fact, Jesus never wants you to do that. Ignoring your feelings, belittling them, or burying them deep down inside, is *exactly* what the enemy wants you to do. He wants you to think that nobody cares about you. God doesn't want that, because it's not the truth! With Him, you are infinitely and *always* loved, no matter how you feel. So instead of suppressing what is bothering you, or making you angry or frustrated—whatever it is that hurts so badly and is causing you pain—examine those feelings and then bring them to God *unashamed*.

Jesus doesn't want us to replay our sad our feelings over and over, while at the same time listing off all of the reasons as to "why" things will never get better. Instead, He wants us to take those feelings and talk to Him about it. He wants us to a*sk* Him for comfort, and *ask* Him for help. Ask, and He will give both to you without measure! (See John 14:26, Ephesians 3:20).

Feeling sorry for ourselves is the fuse which gets lit in our souls that leads to a powder-keg of an explosively miserable life. Self-pity is exactly what Satan wants from you. Why give him his way? Instead of going down the path of "I never get a good break," or, "Just my luck!" or even, "God never answers my prayers!"—you must *begin* to stand on the promises of God! Those promises are found in the Bible! Which brings me to my next point and one of the main features of this book: studying the life of Christ.

Studying Jesus through the Word of God is crucial to having a strong relationship with Him. The Bible from front to back is about Jesus— IT'S HIS STORY. Even before He physically came to earth in the New Testament, Jesus Christ was still the reason *why* the Bible was put together! Ultimately, the Bible is a love story. It's a great masterpiece about the creation of the universe and man, our sinful fall which broke our relationship with God, and then the saving all of mankind *through* Jesus Christ!

What's so great about the Bible is the very words on those pages are now *your* defense against the enemy's evil plans for your life. For example, when you begin to feel sad and you are having a very tough day, because of what you've come to understand from the Bible, you now know that you can talk to God about anything—even if it's your own poor choices that are causing you so many problems. You know *what* He will say based on what you've studied, as well as through what the Holy Spirit speaks to your heart (see Romans 10:17, 12:2).

This is the relationship God longs to have with you! A respectful and *trusting* relationship! As this relationship grows, pity-parties are few and far between because you know how loving your Heavenly Father really is—and you know His words! I've found that the best way to defeat a pity-party is to praise God, especially when you feel like there is nothing to currently praise Him for. Praise Him *anyway*. Trust me, it's like watering a parched flower. You *will* come back to life, and you *will* be rejuvenated! So praise, praise, praise away! Praising is not *just* for God, it's also to make you feel better!

There is one more thing I want to say about the importance of the Bible, and that is to make sure you look at it as a whole. Yes, there are tons of harsh things which happened in the Old Testament, many times God appears mean and cruel. But God is *not* mean or cruel—He doesn't even have that ability. Instead, God is *love* (see 1 John 4:8). He is completely perfect, just, and sovereign. He's incapable of being wrong.

God sees the ultimate outcome of everything, in *every* situation. So sometimes He had to amputate a gangrene toe to keep the entire leg from becoming infected. He had us in mind, you and me, even in the Old Testament. He sees the big picture and we do not.

As New Covenant believers, we must also remember that before Christ died on the Cross, the old Mosaic Covenant with God was built on a law-based works system. That system proved not one single person could ever live up to God's perfect standard (see Romans 3:10, Galatians 3:11). This was the very reason Jesus came to earth—to give us a *new* standard of justification with God by grace through faith (see Ephesians 2:8-9, Romans 5:1).

He saw how badly we were failing and He wanted to help us by completing the life of perfection *for* us! What love that God would actually belittle Himself enough to become one of His very own creations *just* to save us! (See Philippians 2:7-8, 2 Corinthians 5:21).

One of the greatest benefits of being a New Covenant believer is Jesus has finished all of the work *for* us, now, we simply rest (see Hebrews 4:11).

In this state of rest, we can then accomplish more than we ever have before—by grace!

Grace is free. If grace was not free, then it wouldn't be called grace (see Romans 11:6). Grace is completely undeserved, and you have access to God *through* your faith alone in Christ's perfect, finished work. There is no better way to describe this generous act of Jesus', *except* through grace—except through unearned kindness.

This is how good of a God we have, that He would give His one and only perfect Son to us, in order to pay off a debt which otherwise would be un-payable. The Bible says, "the wages of sin is death" (see Romans 6:23). Jesus never sinned, so He didn't deserve to die. We do. Actually, we *did*, before our faith in Christ!

So when you read the Bible believe all of it as the truth from front to back, because it is. Don't just pick apart pieces of it, but instead, read it as a whole. Read it in context. Remember that Jesus *completed* the Bible. Without Him finishing it, the Bible would be an absolute nightmare. When grim things get brought up from the Old Testament, look to the people's actions to determine why such things happened *rather* than seeing God as being a barbarian. Look at the impossibility of living by the Law, and how we needed a new way of grace.

When reading the Bible—especially in the beginning of believing in Jesus—if you still can't understand why certain things were like they were, simply cover it up with the grace of Jesus Christ. Why apply grace to the Old Testament? Because when Jesus came in the flesh, He replaced Old Testament laws with grace (see Hebrews 8:13). Therefore, be sure to apply the New Covenant Jesus-filter to all parts of the Bible. The *how*, *why*, and *what next*, should always have Jesus involved—from Genesis to Revelation. All the Old Testament really does is bring to light just who God is, *impersonally*. Then, in the New Testament, we get to meet God in person! (See John 14:9).

The Bible is full of strange things, customs, wordings, and situations which seem "off" to us in our current generation, but if we can make Jesus the very heart of every Bible study, and get to know Him *first*, the rest of the Bible makes perfect sense. From the pages of this great book I've learned that I *love* Jesus! Christ has taught me that He and I *together*—no matter what or who we face—we can move mountains! We can make a huge difference on this planet and *for* the Kingdom of God! He wants the same for you!

I honestly believe, deep in my heart, that I can help *you* understand God's purpose for your life. He has given me a gift of reaching out to others *through* my typed words. I tried burying this gift for a long time, and I'll talk about that later, but this book is part of my gifting—my calling—I say with complete humility. Some of the stuff I'll say won't always make you feel good, but it will make you think about what Christ wants from you, that's what's most important.

My desire is to help make *your* purpose for living more clear for you! I know I can do this based on my life's experiences and the relationship with Christ I currently have. God uses all of us in many different ways to get things done. I pray that I can interlock my gifts and calling with yours, in order to help you get to know Jesus better. This is why we live and breathe, and where we find our meaning—it's Jesus. *He* is our purpose.

A LITTLE BACKGROUND ON MYSELF

When Mom got pregnant with my older brother Luke in 1979, my dad wanted to name him Scott. But Grandma said, "Oh no, honey. You should give him a name from the Bible." So Mom and Dad let Grandma name him Luke. I've been told this story 136 times over the years, so I know it well. It is also said that Mom and Dad only wanted *one* boy and *one* girl. That was their plan, that was it. But God had other plans. So after Luke was born, the very next year they put in their order for a baby girl, but instead they got twin boys! Mark and me! Imagine that! Dad wanted to name us Benjamin and Brandon, but Grandma said the same thing that she said about Luke's pre-name, Scott, which was, "I don't like it. You should name these two babies from the Bible." She then told Dad, "Just name them Matthew and Mark, and then all you'll need is a John." Dad replied with, "Mom! Please don't say that!"

After Mark and I got here in July of 1981, Mom and Dad tried yet *again* to have the baby girl that they always wanted—but instead they got a fourth boy! My little brother John was named even before he was conceived! It couldn't have been, Matthew, Mark, Luke, and Fred. So Johnny Boy got him a Bible name as well. Oh how I love my brothers…but world beware, by 1983, Matthew, Mark, Luke, and John McMillen, were here to make an impact.

However, Mom and Dad weren't finished just yet! They still wanted a little girl, and they finally got her. In August of 1986, after having four rowdy boys, they mustered-up enough *faith* to have a little girl, so they aptly named her just that, Faith. My brothers, sister, and I are extremely close. In my opinion, much closer than most siblings are. Our bond is very tight, we love each other dearly, and I believe it's because of God's hand on our lives as we grew up in complete turmoil.

"The Big Happy Family" that every little kid dreams of never got off the ground for us. By the time I was in kindergarten, the plague of divorce had hit my family like a Category 5 Hurricane. What ensued thereafter were atrocious custody battles, supervised parental visits, tear-filled sleepless nights in foster homes, 10 different schools, and the hell of living in children's shelters. Eventually, all of us kids were split up like pets, bank accounts, and furniture. Satan started in with his destructive ways very early in my life, but God has used all of it, *all* of it, for my eventual good.

By the time I was twelve, Dad finally got full custody of us. He was, and still is, a very hard worker. But because of the nasty separation, Dad lost absolutely everything he had built up and saved over the years. Legal fees ruined him financially. The divorce pained him in his soul. When he got all of us kids back in 1993, Dad was almost 40. He now had nothing to show for anything any longer because of the hellish custody battle which went on for years. My goodness, what this man went through to get us back, I don't see *how* he went through it. Thinking about it now, it really breaks my heart. I'm sure that on many days he was tempted to end it all, but I'm so glad he didn't.

Now, I'm going to keep my tone respectful and tame as I move forward to talk about my mother. Before I continue on in this book, I need to make clear that my mom had a very rough childhood herself. Her father was not very loving or kind—he was legalistic and harsh. And *her* mom abandoned their family when she was just a little girl, ultimately leaving *my* mom to take her place. Household duties and other adult responsibilities which no child should ever have to deal with was the normal life for Mom. It wasn't fair to her, and she suffered severely because of it.

I understand now, that hurt people *hurt* people—including their own kids. Mom was hurting, in turn, *we* got hurt. She has since apologized deeply to me, and I've completely forgiven her. As of today, we have a somewhat normal mother/son relationship. Further, everything from my childhood is all in the past now. I AM NOT A VICTIM. PERIOD. I don't live there any longer, I'm a grown man living my life in the year 2015, not 1995.

My nightmare of a childhood has made me who I am today, and God has used all of my pain to get me to where I'm currently at in life—so I'm grateful. As silly as it may sound, I don't regret having gone through it. God had a plan and a purpose the entire time, and He never left me! Also, I *have* to show my mom forgiveness because Christ has done the same for me. Forgiveness is a non-negotiable with God. What right do we have to withhold something from others which God gave freely to us? Further, genuine forgiveness is the only way to truly understand and feel the un-conditional love of Christ! Mom, I hope you know that you are completely forgiven. I love you.

However, I am still going to talk about some of the things she put us through as a family. I'm not saying that Dad was perfect by any means, but he was usually loving, comforting, and kind to us kids. I always looked forward to seeing Dad each day, but my maternal relationship was non-existent. I never knew what it was like to feel the true love of a mother. Some of the stuff Mom did was just plain cruel. It was a torment to be her child, you never knew what you were going to get. It wasn't fair or fun or comforting, ever. Not at all. Even if I strain, I can't think of any real length of time that I enjoyed my relationship with Mom. I didn't trust her. I was scared of her. It was not normal. Our relationship wasn't loving or good in any way. As a kid, I always felt like I was a bother to her. I felt hated, disliked, and even despised.

I can remember being in first grade, waking up in the middle of the night from a nightmare and then trying to sneak into my mom's bed. I crawled in very slowly down by her feet so she wouldn't notice I was there, and then she literally *kicked* me off the bed with her feet. So I just laid there on the floor, longing to be kept safe from whatever it was that I was afraid of. I just wanted to be in the same room with her, even if she wouldn't show me any love.

Any type of closeness with Mom was always quickly destroyed by her irrational actions, addictions, and poor choices. She did *not* want to be the mother of us five kids, and it was obvious. When you're little, you think that something is wrong with you when your parent treats you so terribly. Looking back, I wish I could tell my younger self, "The only thing that is wrong here is *her*. *You* are spectacular. Don't you *ever* believe her lies."

When you have a mother who is *so* bitter, and *so* caught up in herself... well, I'll just say this, you will be very fortunate if your family lasts for very long. Like attempting to sweep sand off the beach, Dad trying to get Mom to "be good" and "have a family" was an unwinnable battle. SHE JUST WAS NOT HAVING IT! Jesus wasn't lying when He said Satan comes *only* to "STEAL, KILL, AND DESTROY" (see John 10:10), *that* includes families! I love my mom now, as a grown man, but as a boy I didn't love her at all. I *wanted* to love my mom, I also wanted to *be* loved by her, but that just wasn't in the hand of cards I was dealt.

As I got older, I finally learned that I didn't *have* to accept unacceptable behavior from her just because she was my mom. Her fear tactics, rage, and guilt trips stopped working on me. God finally taught me that *I* have to be okay, even if *she's* not.

But marriages, and families in general, are some of the devil's main targets to attack and destroy. COMPLETE DEVASTATION would be the best way to describe the condition of my family growing up *because* of divorce. That divorce was caused by selfishness, self-centeredness, no resistance to temptation, no respect of boundaries, refusal to forgive and love as Christ co commands, and absolutely *no* reverence for God. When you don't love people like Christ loves you, including your own family, then it's only a matter of time before that relationship is destroyed or seriously injured.

By the time Dad got us back in 1993, we were almost at poverty level so Grandma moved in to help us out. *She* raised all of us kids, not Mom. Grandma took on the five of us as her own, as well as every other kid in the neighborhood. As Dad worked 70+ hours a week trying to catch up on bills and pay people back, all the while attempting to make enough money to feed and clothe us, Grandma stepped up and stood in the gap for my mother—while Mom did nothing.

Running us around constantly, cooking, cleaning, and doing her best to corral and guide five kids, *she* was our mother—Mom was gone, nowhere to be found. Her addictions were more important than us. Dad, however, never did get back on his feet. Even to this day in his sixties, he is still playing catch-up from what that divorce did to his life.

I do want to point out and say something very special about my dad. Besides his tremendous work ethic—which I inherited—and his great love for us kids, he also instilled in me the idea of *grace*. I never knew how much I would need God's grace until I was in my thirties. It was then that the seeds of grace Dad planted in me finally sprouted up and out. I'll be forever thankful to Dad for teaching me this. Another thing I learned from him, which has had a very positive impact on my life is this: *I never once heard him complain.*

Even when he would be worn out from working all day, hobbling through the back door way past dark, he always had a very pleasant, loving attitude toward us. No matter what the house looked like or what chaos going on, it was always good to see Dad. Although he got the short end of the stick in regard to his marriage, he was so proud and happy to finally have us back at home—even if he didn't get to enjoy us as much as he wanted to because of having to work so much. Thank you, Dad, for all you've done for me. I love you.

But because Dad worked his fingers to the bone, usually seven days a week, we didn't get to see much of him. In high school, when basketball season rolled around each year, I'd look up into the stands during my games and *my* mom and dad weren't there like the other kids' were. This was very difficult for me, especially as I was trying to transition from a boy into a young man. I so wanted to see Mom and Dad sitting together and cheering for me, maybe having a Coke and some popcorn while enjoying each other's company…but…Mom and Dad were *not* getting back together, and Dad, he had to work. He'd make it to my games "if he got time"… he never got time. Then again, I shouldn't say never. He might have come to a few of my games, but I never counted on it. That hurt really bad.

Dad was usually gone each day before dawn. We rarely got to see him in the mornings, and we were lucky to get to see him in the evenings *if* he got home by 9:00 or 10:00. Every once in a while he'd get home by 6:00 or 7:00—maybe once or twice a week—*maybe*. So usually when he got home, I was already in bed. I really loved my dad and wanted to have him home at a decent time on a daily basis. You know, to hang out and do stuff with? Maybe have dinner together and have some conversations? But that didn't happen very often, it just wasn't part of my childhood. However, if I *was* in bed when he got home late, he'd come into my room, kiss me on the head, and tell me that he loved me. Which I'm sure he did. But spending *time* with your kids shows them love, not just a peck on the head. Dad didn't understand that.

I know he had to work, but as a man I've molded my own work schedule into making sure I'm home at a good time each day *because* of Dad's failure to do so. It took me coming to know Jesus deeper before this was so important to me, but maybe that's because He brought to light just how bad it feels to not have your dad home each night. It doesn't feel good at all. Although I've failed in the past, I don't want Grace to feel like work is more important than she is. My family *needs* me at home. Just my presence as "Dad" is immeasurably important. Workaholism effects many families very negatively, not mine any longer.

We all knew Dad was doing his best, but that didn't change the fact that there was severe pain in our home. There was a complete lack of discipline, no personal responsibly or accountability, organization was nonexistent—and this was all because Dad was an absentee parent most of the time. Grandma always tried to defend Dad and keep things positive, but even she knew it was not okay that he was hardly ever home.

Eventually Dad became a slave to work and you could never convince him otherwise...*that's* where he found his identity, work. Even if he would not admit it, the proof was in the pudding. Or as Jesus would say, "A tree is known by its fruit" (Luke 6:44). All Dad did was work, and don't you *dare* say anything about it, or else you would be looked at as ungrateful or disrespectful. The fact was, I *was* grateful, but I still wanted Dad home regularly. Looking back, the hidden manipulation that occurred, as if it was not okay for me to think that Dad worked too much, was wrong. This was a boundary of mine that he refused to respect left scars on my soul.

His addiction to work and being gone from home had a seriously *negative* effect on my life, as well as the lives of my siblings. Mark, Luke, John, or Faith, might not ever say it, but we all wanted Dad home much more than he was while growing up. This bothered us greatly. It would have been *so nice* to have a normal, happy family, but that didn't happen. What God *did* allow to happen in my childhood was part of a much *greater* good than I can possibly fathom. I'm thankful for the grace He gave me to be able to endure it.

With Grandma in her late sixties and doing most of the raising, it was basically a free-for-all at the McMillen House. It was absolute nuts. Mom was out of the picture by her own choice, and Dad was working, so Grandma began to take care of us, when really, she should have been enjoying her Golden Years. I've learned *not* to say that to her though because she'll tell me, "It was an honor to get to raise you kids!" And we were bad! I mean, *I wasn't*, but the rest were!

Even now, Grandma will say, "Baby, I wouldn't have had it any other way. I really enjoyed being there for you all." She really *was* my mom, but she would never dare disrespect my real mom by saying that. After everything Mom put us through, not *once* did Grandma *ever* bad-mouth her—not one time! If *anyone* deserved to be bitter toward Mom, or felt like they had a right to hate her, Grandma could have easily been at the top of that list. When Dad asked her to move in and help, Grandma could have told him, "I've already raised my kids, I'm not raising any more," but she didn't. Instead, she stepped up, and like Dad, she never complained or quit on us. Even more importantly, she never made us kids feel like we didn't deserve to have her there. The positive spiritual impact this had on me was *enormous*.

My mom abandoned us several times, but back then, Grandma never allowed us to use Mom's poor choices as an excuse to hate her. Any time I began to voice my personal hate toward Mom, Grandma would correct me and say, "Matthew, that's your mother, so you need to respect her no matter what. Don't you say that about her again." But I didn't want to hear it! NOBODY ELSE HAD A MOM LIKE MINE! IT WAS NOT FAIR!

As a young teenager, sometimes I would go into an angry tantrum of just how bad of a mom *my* mom was. I would spout off horrible names about her because of my severe hurt and frustration. But Grandma never threw fuel on that fire in me. Instead, she would say, "Son, I love your mother very much. She gave me five grandkids. You need to love her too." But I *didn't* love her, at all! SHE DIDN'T DESERVE MY LOVE! Besides the woman birthing me, Mom gave me *no* reason to love her! No reason whatsoever! The pain she caused me was MASSIVE!...*This* was my young mindset.

I never knew what the caress of a loving mother felt like. Grandma tried, but Grandma was still "just my grandma," not my mom. I wanted my *mom*. Of course, now at 34, I have no harsh feelings toward her at all. I'm free from what the devil tried so desperately to cause in my life *through* my mother's actions. Which is hate, resentment, bitterness, blame, anger, and unforgiveness—those things do *not* describe me as a child of God (see Galatians 5:22-23).

This took some serious mind renewal on my part, as well as *choosing* to not walk by the flesh, but by my spirit (see Galatians 5:16, Romans 8:9). But when I was a kid I didn't *want* to forgive her, I was very mad at her for what she did to our family; eventually, I was disgusted by her. Grandma, on the other hand, would continue to say to me, "Matthew, you need to forgive your mom. She is still your mother, no matter what." Unbeknownst to me at the time, Grandma was teaching me the love of Jesus Christ.

What an absolute blessing it was being raised by my Grandma! When I think about it, I feel blessed to have her blood running through my veins! I cannot emphasize with my typed words just how fortunate we were to have her in our home. We didn't realize it at the time, but Grandma was planting seeds in our souls each day which would last a lifetime. Little by little, she was instilling in each of us a deep hunger, love, and respect for God. When I look back, it baffles me at the amount of sacrificial strength and dedication she had toward us, Dad, and even Mom.

And yeah, I know that most people think *their* grandma is the greatest, but mine really is! I'm telling you the truth! God doesn't make 'em like her anymore! I guess if I were forced to compare her to somebody else, personality wise, it would probably be Miss Kay from *Duck Dynasty*—just so darn sweet! Even now, at 86, she is so much fun to be around. I *still* learn some kind of wisdom from every conversation we have.

With Grandma leading us, we got to see and *feel* what the true love of Christ really is! Friends, I'm talking unconditional love for absolutely everyone—NO MATTER WHAT! Another thing Grandma did which was a catalyst for showing me Christ, was the fact that I *never* heard her gossip. I never even heard her say so much as a foul word about what most would consider "despicable people." She sees everyone how Jesus sees them, which is with eyes of love, respect, hope, and potential. When you visit my grandma, she always has something good to say about you right away. Even if you don't think there's anything good to say about yourself, she'll *find* something—almost immediately—to build you up and make you feel good. She personifies Christ almost perfectly.

What she taught me back then is now what is allowing me to write this book today! If it weren't for Grandma, not only would I *not* be writing this, I would not be who I am. Who knows where I'd be or what kind of trouble I'd be *in*, without her. She literally saved my life by allowing Jesus to live through her and by being a loving example to me.

By doling out her Godly wisdom on a regular basis, I got to know who Jesus is. Grandma quoted Scripture to me *all* the time, back then I didn't know why, but now I do. It was because she knew I would need God more than anything else in my life as an adult. The Bible says to "train up a child in the way that they should go, and when they are old, they will not depart from it" (Proverbs 22:6). She knew this and she did *just* that. Raising us was part of her purpose!

But maybe the very best thing about Grandma is that she actually *showed* us who Jesus is. She showed us what unconditional love looks like! She didn't just say it or talk about it, and she didn't demand that *we* do it— SHE LIVED IT! Furthermore, she never had any excuses about anything, and she never had any blame! No matter how badly someone took advantage of her or did her wrong, she always covered up their sin with her love. My grandfather, her husband, was an alcoholic. He was also a philanderer, mostly angry, extremely selfish, and just about the very opposite of who my Grandma is—but she still refused to leave him.

He died in 1994 but even after that she never talked bad about him, not once. Sure, she was truthful about the sorry life he lived. She didn't sugarcoat it. But even then, she still spoke respectfully about him despite my grandfather causing her more pain than absolutely anyone else ever did. He didn't deserve her, she deserved *so* much better. But she was committed to him for better or worse, until death did them part. There was nothing that Grandpa or anyone else could do to change her mind about her commitment to him. After he died she never married again, and even though she was never treated like the queen she really is, she still lived up to her vows to both Grandpa and to God. This undying commitment she had to her husband became more and more inspirational to me as I got older—as the years went by in my own marriage.

Although Grandma was extremely loving, she didn't disregard the truth! It wasn't "anything goes," it was, "We stand on the truth of the Bible." So *truth* was taught as well. Of course, I didn't like this when I was young, but I sure do now. If I only knew just how sweet the truth really was at an earlier age in life, I would have decided to let Jesus live through me much sooner. Had I done so, it would have saved me tons of heartache, trouble, fear, addiction, and pain.

One last thing I'll say about Grandma for now, is that she *also* showed us what confidence in Christ looks like! SHE WAS A FIRM LADY! Not some old pushover! Yet, she still loved us no matter what. That deep down confidence on the inside of her came from her faith in Jesus. She'll be the first one to tell you that. She knew who always backed her up, and it showed. I'll forever love her, and I'll forever thank her for all she's done for me. Thank you, Grandma. Thank you, thank you, thank you. I love you.

Now that you know a little bit more about me, I feel like you should also know that I don't think I'm better than anyone else. I'm a just like you, a human. No matter where you are at in life *we* are equal in the eyes of God. How? Because He has a never-ending love for each of us which will never go away! (See Jeremiah 31:3, Romans 5:8, John 3:16).

And when we get to know Jesus *deeper*, we get to know God's never-ending love for us, deeper. So thank you for joining me! My prayer is that I can help you go further into *your* relationship with Jesus Christ, by simply telling you about *my* personal journey of doing the same thing! So let's go!

Part One

WE BEGIN, WITH OURSELVES

Chapter 1

───────※───────

SELF-HELP AND PRAYER

*"...be transformed by the renewing of your mind.
Then you will be able to test and approve what God's
will is—his good, pleasing and perfect will."*

See ROMANS 12:2

SELF-HELP DOES NOT EXIST

There is a very common myth that goes like this: "God helps those who help themselves," and that's not true. As a matter of fact, just the *opposite* is true. God helps those who admit that they *can't* possibly help themselves. Yes, God does help even those who don't believe in Him, to an extent, but when you step into your relationship with Christ, you unlock God-given favor that you did not have access to before. This favor begins by Him blessing you with a peace and confidence in yourself *through* Christ *rather* than simply by your own human abilities.

What follows next is Him developing your *human* abilities *for* Him, *through* your relationship *with* Him. You no longer have to muster up enough self-made determination to help yourself each day—all the pressure is off! Instead, you depend on Him for absolutely everything. In return, He teaches you how to accomplish feats *through* His grace, resulting in spiritual fruit being grown in your life (see Galatians 5:22-23). Let me explain how this works because it took me over 30 years to figure this out—to find this *sweet spot* in life, this, *resting* in God's grace. It's pretty great!

If you go to your local Barnes & Noble Bookstore, or search online, there are literally thousands of self-help books on the market. I want to make perfectly clear that this is *not* a self-help book. I, personally, own my own, do not have the ability to help you, help yourself. Many authors have attempted to do this and I've even purchased some of their books. Now don't get me wrong, their books are valuable and have some very helpful information. They lay out practical plans and give you helpful tools to *attempt* to achieve self-help, and some are very good!

I've found myself attempting to apply principles from self-help books to my own life and they are usually very helpful, but only for a while. But the problem is, as humans, no matter how hard we try, we *cannot* help ourselves. It's impossible.

God knows this because He made us this way—so *He* is here to help! God is well aware that *something* is missing in each and every one of us which removes our ability to help ourselves. We don't have it in us, genetically or spiritually, to achieve such a task. We can put forth a really, *really* good effort, but helping ourselves without the actual help from *who* created us is futile.

We *need* our Creator's input on *us*. We can't get this from ourselves because we didn't *make* ourselves. All of us have a built-in desire to understand from our Maker just *how* we can possibly live out our lives in the way He designed them to be lived. This God-given desire is there and it will never go away (see Ecclesiastes 3:11). No matter how much we try to ignore it, God's fingerprints are all over us.

Thankfully, when we begin to allow Jesus to live through us, we don't even have to *try* to help ourselves any longer. His help allows our efforts to be strain-free. Through Him, it's almost as if living our life is easy, even when it's extremely difficult. Why is this? Because we are simply being the branch who is connected to the vine—Jesus (see John 15:5). Branches don't strain, stress, or worry. They get all of their life from the vine.

Understanding this breeds confidence in us! Enjoying "being a branch" is based on knowing God's unconditional love for you. In turn, trust in your relationship with Him is built. So no matter what—or who—He allows in your life, because of *Christ's* life in you, you stay at peace (see Philippians 4:7). When unfair situations arise and people hurt you, God *helps* you *because* you are connected to Him. So we take the blow and don't fret *knowing* that we don't even *have* to help ourselves. Rather, we simply do everything we possibly *can* do and then trust God to take care of the rest. This gives us peace.

Once we begin living our lives depending on God's help, rather than on self-help, everything clicks into place. That void in our life is finally filled up. A relationship with God makes you feel like a fish swimming in water, or a bird flying high in the sky…it's just…*natural*. It's what you were created to do!

As for all of the books on how to find help for your inner-self, inner-me, or to develop your inner-winner, they will ultimately leave you feeling empty and searching for a different style of self-help book—yet again. The reading material that is currently out there on how to help yourself be positive, productive, more enthusiastic, or how to be truly happy, all of them are missing the key ingredient to true self-help which is actually *surrendering from helping ourselves*. These books are also missing the Star! The main character of the greatest book of all time! The Omnipotent One who has finished all of the hard work *for* us! Our #1 Source of help! Our Vine!…*Jesus*. Jesus, in Spirit, is called *the Helper* (see John 14:26). He is who we need.

Friend, if you could help yourself you would have done it by now. Self-help is not real. We need Jesus' help with our lives, and in order to have access to this help, we don't have to do anything more than surrender our desire to help ourselves. This is *hard*, but this is possible! (See Philippians 4:13). Remember, branches don't help themselves, they get all of their efforts from the vine! All they gotta do is *be* a branch!

Graveyards are full of people who never figured this out. They tried everything *on their own* which they *thought* would help them with their lives. Money, sex, fame, work, honor, charity, greed, church, alcohol, drugs, food, power, women, men, boyfriends, girlfriends, husbands, wives, affairs, kids, cars, porn, gambling, hobbies, physical fitness, vacations, *you name it*, it's all been tried before—and it's all *fleeting*. It's all temporary. None of that stuff is coming from the vine, it's not eternal. *Only* our relationship with God is! This is why God created inside of you a feeling of incompleteness *without* a relationship with Him. You *feel* incomplete without Him because you *are* incomplete without Him.

All of us have a God-shaped hole in our souls that can only be filled in perfectly by Him. Nobody else can fill it, and *nothing* else can fill it. We were made to be completed by God alone. The good news is, once we finally enter into this relationship with Him we can fully enjoy our lives and everything else in it! (See John 10:10). When we get our relationship with God set first—which is a *very* healthy relationship—we can then have other healthy relationships as well. We can have relationships with *people* which are built on our relationship with *God*, not the other way around.

When we have our relationship with God first in our lives we will then have the ability to walk by His Spirit in us *rather* than by the flesh (see Galatians 5:16). Also, this relationship begins to transform our mindsets into that of His (see Romans 12:2). This is why Jesus said, "Seek first the kingdom of God and his righteousness, and everything else will be provided to you as well" (Matthew 6:33). What Jesus was saying is, "Put me first, then I'll give you everything else you need."

Sure, we can try and try and *try* to help ourselves but it will never happen permanently. No matter what we do or how put-together we may seem, until we actually stop trying to help ourselves we can't receive the help we need from our Creator—from our vine. Jesus explained it well when He said, "Whoever finds their life will lose it, and whoever loses their life for my sake will find it" (Matthew 10:39).

This is the very *beginning* of your purpose. It all begins by admitting you can't do anything about your current condition on your own—and that only Jesus can. After that admission, we become empowered because our old sinful spirit dies and we get a new *perfect* spirit! (See Romans 6:6, 2 Corinthians 5:17). From then on everything you do is *because* of Christ and it's *through* Christ! You are no longer your own and that's a great relief! (See Galatians 2:20, 1 Corinthians 6:20).

Once you finally humble yourself enough to admit this, both to yourself and to God, *then* your entire life changes. You become the branch you were created to be and you get a whole new identity: *child of God*! (See John 1:12, Galatians 3:26). It's not just *you* any longer inside your body! It's you combined with Jesus! (See 1 Corinthians 6:19, Colossians 3:3). You begin to take on *His* characteristics, *His* truth, and *His* ways, and your real life begins! You start to experience *real* joy, *real* peace, *real* confidence, and *real* hope! (See Galatians 5:22-23).

However, this is still a choice. *Could* God force you into a relationship with Him? I'm sure He could, He's God. He can do anything He wants. But He loves you way too much to force you to love Him back. And what is love if it's not chosen? It's not real. It's fake. It's a duty.

This is why God gave you free will. Free will allows you have the ability to decide *if* you want to love Him back. Yes, God wants you to love Him, this is why He made you to *need* Him. But just because you need something that doesn't always mean you want it. God allows you to choose to do whatever you want—even if it's not what you need. This includes stepping into a close relationship with Him through coming to know Jesus Christ deeply. *You* gotta want it. You already *need* it—admit it or not—we all do. But do you want it? For me that answer is a resounding "Yes!" I *wanted* a relationship with Jesus Christ and I've got it! Because of that, I've got all the help I'll ever need. No self-help required.

IT ALL BEGINS WITH PRAYER

So maybe you've decided to act on this need for help which God has placed in you—*you want it*. That's awesome! Congratulations because now you've got it! So what's next? First things first: *Pray*. Pray all the time. When you pray, all you're doing is talking to God inwardly or outwardly. Prayer is easy, it's just chit-chatting with God. *Religion* has made prayer complicated, but prayer is simply talking to God, who lives *in* you.

Jesus gives you the right to talk to God about anything. The Bible says you can approach God with confidence! (See Hebrews 4:16). Your behavior and attitudes—good or bad—do not determine whether or not God hears your prayers. So never think you're not holy enough to talk to God, because you are!

As a Christian, your perfect spirit is not only *holy* but it is blameless and free from accusation (see Colossians 1:22). You are allowed to say whatever you want to God, *whenever* you want to God, *wherever* you want to God—and your body doesn't have to be in any certain position. He's your loving Father, and loving Fathers care about their kids. They aren't concerned over whether or not their kids are kneeling in front of them. You don't need a special robe or dress-code to talk to your Father, you don't need a degree, and you don't need to be in any special room, building, or geographical location.

None of that stuff makes you any more important to God. He simply wants you to be real with Him at all times. Nothing is too big or too small to talk to Him about because you've been adopted into His family! (See Ephesians 1:5). YOU ARE NOW PART OF HIS HOUSEHOLD! Because of your new spirit you are no longer a foreigner or separated from Him! (See Ephesians 2:19). So never be afraid to talk! Prayer is simply talking to your Dad, and your Dad wants to have a loving, respectful, *trusting* relationship with you, through prayer.

Prayer is so simple! It's not about chanting long, eloquent, memorized phrases, it's about communicating. In order to begin a relationship with anyone, you must communicate with them. You must get to know them. When you communicate with God, you don't need to start throwing out *thees* and *thous* and *shalt nots*. No, you don't have to talk like that because you don't live in the 16th century. Just talk normal. Just communicate. Just get to know Him. That's prayer.

———

"TALK TO GOD LIKE HE IS YOUR BEST FRIEND, A LOVING FATHER, A MENTOR, A COMFORTER, OR A COACH."

———

Talk to God like He is your best friend, a loving father, a mentor, a comforter, or a coach. Just talk. Just pray. It could be out loud or to yourself, that doesn't matter. Your prayer doesn't even have to be pieced together in words. It could just be a string of thoughts that you are directing *toward* Him. You could be in church when you pray, or in bed, or driving (keep your eyes open though). You could be at work, at the gym, at school, it could even be during a pick-up game of basketball. It doesn't matter, just pray! Just talk.

You can pray on the ball field or at practice. You could be in court or sitting across the table from your spouse's divorce lawyer. Pray. Talk to God. You could pray in the middle of a heated argument with someone or even on your death-bed. You can pray in the ICU room or before a job interview, you can pray before a big sales appointment or during a demanding presentation. You could be lying on the couch watching TV or trying to fight off the fleshly urge of an addiction. Pray. You could be drunk as a skunk or high as a kite. Pray. You could be in a night club, a strip joint, or at a crack house. Pray. You could even be watching porn or fighting the temptation to have an affair. God wants you to pray! He wants you to talk to Him! YOU DO NOT SURPRISE HIM! He wants you to ask for help with whatever you are currently involved with or facing! So pray away!

Whether you are heartbroken from a cheating boyfriend or girlfriend, or feeling absolutely worthless and distraught because your parents abandoned you—pray. You could be holding a cold gun up to your mouth or tightening the noose to take your own life. Pray. God wants you to simply say, "Help me." He wants you to *pray*.

You can even pray while sitting at the bar, sad, depressed, and lonely, trying to act as if nothing's wrong, as you laugh with another fellow drunk.

Pray. You could be getting dressed at your mistress' house or in a hotel room. Pray.

You could be celebrating your sobriety date! Pray! "Thank you, God! Thank you for so much strength!" You could be witnessing the birth of your child or walking your daughter down the isle. Pray. "Thank you, Jesus. You are so good to me." You could be expanding your company into another state or buying that beautiful sports car or home you've always dreamed of…yes, pray. Tears could be flowing down your face because you've finally come to understand God's love for you in Christ…pray. "Thank you. Thank you for this gift." God *longs* for you to talk to Him, through prayer.

When Paul said, "Pray without ceasing" (1 Thessalonians 5:17), this is what he was talking about. He was saying we should live out our lives with an *attitude* of prayer, all day, every day. So begin speaking to God today, in *all* of your circumstances whether good, bad, or indifferent. He is waiting for you! Simply say, "Help me," or "Thank you," or "Show me how," or "I need you." A go-to prayer for me is this: "What do you want me to do?" I also pray such things as, "Give me the strength to do this," "Please, use me," as well as, "Help me. Help me. Help me."

Just say something. Just say *anything*. It's not so much what you say that matters as it is you are actually talking to God. He cares deeply for you and He already knows what you need, even before you ask (see Matthew 6:8). But He still wants you to ask. He still wants you to talk to Him. He still wants you to pray. God wants to be included in absolutely every part of your life! He wants to be there for you! He wants to help you! He wants to lead you, guide you, and protect you! He's in you and He's not going anywhere (see 2 Timothy 2:13), so speak up.

"PRAYER IS SIMPLY A ONE-ON-ONE CONVERSATION WITH THE CREATOR OF THE UNIVERSE."

Prayer is simply a one-on-one conversation with the Creator of the universe. It's simply talking to who made you, and who loves you. Prayer gets God deeply involved in your choices and mindsets, so talk to Him all the time! He *will* talk back to you! It might not be in an actual, audible voice—although it could be—but God mostly speaks to our spirits. It's just a *knowing* we have because we are connected to Him, and this knowing doesn't always agree with you.

Friend, when you pray God doesn't always break out a big flashing arrow, pointing in the direction you should go. You don't always hear, "This is the correct choice. Do this." Instead, you simply pray, *listen*, and then trust that you are making the correct choice based on that prayer. The Holy Spirit then *guides* your choices so that all of them will eventually work out for good—somehow, someway—even if you never get to see those results on this side of heaven! (See Romans 8:28). So if you haven't started yet, begin praying today!

Chapter 2

MORE THAN ANYTHING ELSE, GOD CARES ABOUT YOUR HEART

"Blessed are the pure in heart, for they will see God." –Jesus

MATTHEW 5:8

"Guard your heart above all else, for it determines the course of your life."

PROVERBS 4:23

MY LIFE WAS ROTTEN BECAUSE I IGNORED JESUS

As a Christian, you have a new heart—a new spirit. From the very moment you first believed, your old spirit died *with* Christ, it was buried, and then it was resurrected as a brand-new *perfect* spirit (see Romans 6:6, Ezekiel 3:26, 2 Corinthians 5:17). Christians are not dirty sinners, we *used* to be. The word "sinner" doesn't describe us at all. Also, we do not have a wicked, sinful heart—that is a myth. The reason this myth has been developed is because we have confused our "who" with our "do."

Who are we? We are perfect, holy, *blameless* children of God—spirits! We are heaven-ready and at complete peace with our Creator! (See

Colossians 1:22, John 1:12, Ephesians 1:5, Romans 5:1). We've been for-given of all our sin once and for all! That's past, present, and even future sins! (See Hebrews 10:10, 1 Peter 3:18). However, we still have a physical body called flesh which houses a parasite called sin, as well as unrenewed, old mindsets. This is where our sinful actions and attitudes come from, they do *not* come from us. We are perfect spirits (see Romans 7:5, 8:9, 12:2).

Just because our spirits are perfect that doesn't mean we can't *choose* to walk by what we are dead to: *the sin of the flesh* (see Galatians 5:16, Romans 6:11). Our flesh has a supernatural tumor in it *called* sin. At any time—day or night—we can entertain sin by acting on its desires. It even influences our thoughts through our physical brain (see Romans 7:17, Genesis 4:7). Again, our flesh isn't sinful, but the desires in it stirred up by sin *can* be.

However, it doesn't end there. The sin in our flesh isn't our only problem as a perfect spirit. We also have *unrenewed mindsets*—that is, thoughts and at-titudes which must be reshaped *by* our perfect spirit which is interwoven with God's Spirit (see Romans 12:2, Philippians 4:8, Colossians 3:3). This takes time as we grow each day by going deeper into our relationship with Christ.

I figured this out first hand. By the world's standards, I was a decent person. I helped people, I did my best to provide for my family, and I was living a respectable life. But even through my very best efforts to be a "good person" I was *still* not who God wanted me to be—in my actions and attitudes—and I knew it. Yes, I had accepted the forgiveness of my sins from Jesus when I was a boy. I got my new spirit and I was ready to grow spiritual fruit. But it wasn't until my early thirties that I began to give Him complete access to everything in my life. He was in me, but I still ignored Him. My life was rotten because I refused to walk by my perfect spirit and I wouldn't allow God to renew my mind.

Was I a nice guy? Sure, I thought so. Was I courteous, giving, and well-mannered? More often than not, yes. Was I lazy? Oh heck no. I was the *opposite* of lazy. I was extremely self-motivated, a leader. I was aggressive in all aspects of life. I was driven to succeed and I didn't need anyone to spur me on. I did it myself...or so I thought.

But even with my first-rate attempts of being an upright citizen who worked hard for his family, took care of his health, all the while pursuing the American Dream, I *still* had a rotten life. The day I had this epiphany it was like a light exploded on the inside of me! *"My life is rotten! I'm full of pride! I'm a terrible person!"* When I said that, Jesus didn't agree with me. Instead, He *corrected* me. "You're not full of pride and you're not a terrible person. You are holy and you are good, just like me. However, you are choosing to walk in a manner that doesn't match up with your true identity. I'll help you change this if you let me." I decided to let Him. I decided to allow Him to start living *through* me.

As Christians, I believe what gets us to this point in our lives is not so much through hearing constant preaching or by someone's repeated attempts to make us feel bad. I think we have to finally come to the end of our *own* efforts before we can possibly let God live through us. After we've "tried it all out" and heavily pursued what we *thought* would fulfill our needs, we will eventually come to know how the prodigal son felt as he looked forward to eating with pigs (see Luke 15:16). We find ourselves licking our wounds and telling God, "I'm sorry, I really need your help."

The good news is, the prodigal son never *stopped* being his father's son! Even with all of his poor choices his DNA remained the same and he was *still* a part of that family! This is why the father didn't scold him upon his return, but instead *celebrated* his lifestyle repentance! But even if the prodigal didn't return home to live the life he was born to live, he would have *still* died *as* his father's son. His actions and attitudes never changed *who* he was born of—but instead, his actions and attitudes were ruining his life! His dad had a better plan for him! This is why his father embraced him! (See Luke 15:11-32).

This is what our Heavenly Father does for us. As believers, He knows that we will make choices that do not match up with our heavenly heritage, *but* He will never tell us we are not His kids—ever. Friend, you can't be un-born from God, just the same as you can't be un-born from your earthly parents. Your birth is complete! (See 2 Timothy 2:13, John 1:12, Ephesians 1:5, 1 John 3:9).

So hopefully, like the prodigal, sooner than later we have our come-to moment and see that God's way really is the best way, *and* that it is also *our* way. As we do this, we can finally see that He only wanted the best for us all along.

God wants us to fully allow the Spirit of Christ to live through us—everything about Him. *He* begins to transform our attitudes and actions into *His*. Little by little He begins to remodel everything about us, for the better! Our *do* starts to match up with our *who*! In the beginning of allowing this to happen in my life, the sin of my flesh and my unrenewed mindsets took a pummeling! Both fought Jesus, hard:

"You want me to do *what?*"
"You want me to say *that?*"
"You want me to go *there?*"
"You want me to give *that* up too?"
"You want me to be kind to *them?*"
"You want me to give *more* than 10%?"
"You want me to *not* do anything about *that?*"
"You want me to forgive even *them? That* many times?"
"You want me to keep my mouth shut *again?!*"
"C'MON! YOU'RE KILLING ME, SMALLS!"

...on and on, Jesus was *chipping* and *chipping* and chipping away at the sinful habits of my flesh and mind! It hurt very badly! I THOUGHT I WASN'T GOING TO BE ABLE TO STAND IT! I'M TELLING YOU, I WAS IN *EXCRUCIATING* PAIN! But Jesus was straitening things out. Although it hurt so bad, it also felt so good. Jesus was molding me on the *outside* what was already in me on the *inside*. My rotten life was becoming brand new, and I was letting Jesus do this!

Our lives become rotten because we don't let our true identity shine. This is why Paul said, "For the creation waits in eager expectation for the children of God to be revealed" (Romans 8:19). WE ARE HERE! We are God's children! We must begin to *show* his creation who we really are! Our lives show nastiness when we choose to walk by the flesh, and when we refuse to let the Holy Spirit renew our minds.

You've heard the saying "brain-washed," right? Well that's what we actually need to let Him do! We need to allow the Spirit of God in us to wash our minds clean of who we aren't! Paul was right when he said, "Just as you *have received* Jesus, so *walk* in him" (see Colossians 2:6, my emphasis added).

Although I was very successful in business and "life," I was still *living* my life as a complete failure because of my refusal to walk in my Christian identity. Instead, I walked in extreme anger, blame, addictions, frustration, and fear. I needed some serious help with developing a *new* life. I wanted a peaceful, joyous, *confident* life, so I let Jesus get to work!

Once I gave Him the go-ahead, Christ began to remodel everything around me! He broke out His heavenly tool-belt and started to demolish my rotten life! It was very painful! He started flipping tables, and yelling at demons! "Leave him alone!" Then, He completely choked out my addictions! He put His foot on the throat of my fears! He massacred my legalism! He destroyed my prideful attitude, STOMPED ON IT, and kicked it out! My reputation? He snatched it up and said, "I OWN THIS!" After that, He started *whipping* my jealousy and frustrations with a chain—AND THEN HE SET UP SHOP!...He sat down, and spoke: "Thank you, Matthew. Thank you for letting me do this. I can now fulfill my great plans for you."

RELIGION DESTROYS, RELATIONSHIP HEALS

Jesus was a big proponent of how important the inside of us should look rather than the outside. He told the self-righteous religious Pharisees they were like "white washed tombs with dead bones inside," going on to say, "everything looks beautiful on the outside, but inside everything is dead" (see Matthew 23:27). Jesus was trying to get the point across to these people—who had no real love inside them—by basically saying, "You've got all of these rules and regulations, you even *look* the part of someone who is supposed to be godly, but you still don't know who I am. Therefore, what you do and don't do, and how you look, isn't worth anything."

How many stiff, unloving, religious people do you know like that? When I say "religious," what I'm talking about is being legalistic and lacking empathy. There are so many devout church-goers and church leaders who have Jesus all wrong—they've got the *gospel* all wrong. The gospel is not a behavior improvement program. It's a spiritual death and resurrection. Some people go to church all the time, but they still have no clue about the heart of God or what has really happened inside of them once they believed. Their unrenewed mindsets cause them to think, *"I'm better in the eyes of God than other Christians because I go to church three times a week, and they only go twice."* Or, *"I'm not going to hell and they are because they curse all the time, and I only curse a few times a year."*

These types of Christians exude no unconditional love for others and they are shallow as a creek. They are fair-weather friends and they will kick you out of their circle if you don't do what they say. Their Bibles are full of highlights, notes, and bulletins, but their unrenewed mindsets are void of the deep love of Jesus Christ. They are on the worship team at church, but they'll gossip about anyone who'll listen at lunch. They don't care about what Jesus cares about and they insist on people seeing them tithe. They love to point out the most obvious hypocrites in the church, but truth be told, it's them. Their idle talk consumes them and *religion* is their god.

"..."THEY LOVE TO POINT OUT THE MOST OBVIOUS HYPO-CRITES IN THE CHURCH, BUT TRUTH BE TOLD, IT'S THEM."

Friend, God wants us to go to church so we can learn about Jesus with other believers. He also wants us there so we can help one another. Yes, we can and *should* learn about Him on our own, all the time. But church attendance should still be a priority—not a law—but something that is important to you simply because you love God and people.

However, you don't *have* to go to church to be a Christian or even step foot in an actual building, not one time. Our salvation is not based on anything we do or don't do, but on what Jesus has done and our belief in it. Frankly, the teaching at some churches can actually do more harm than good. You should never leave church feeling scared, disturbed, pressured, or hurt. God doesn't work that way, Satan does (Romans 5:9, 2 Timothy 1:7, 1 Corinthians 14:33).

God *lovingly* corrects us even when we blatantly ignore what He is trying to convict us of. Just look at Jesus' example of correcting His disciples. The only thing you should fear is a life and death *without* Christ— that's it. If a person has not accepted Jesus' forgiveness *that's* a healthy fear. Being eternally separated from God will be *very* bad, to say the least. Living out your short life on planet earth not knowing your Creator intimately, that should make your shudder and feel alone. Be afraid of that. We *need* Christ's forgiveness! We *need* to be joined with Him in spirit right now! (See 2 Corinthians 5:20, 6:2).

But once you get past that point and you've received your new spirit, don't allow the religious people at church to make you feel afraid. God's love for you is perfect and there is no fear to be had from Him as His child. Fear has to do with punishment and Jesus already took your punishment away at the Cross (see 1 John 4:8, Romans 8:1, John 3:17). If fear is the cornerstone of your church, run. Please, don't be afraid any longer.

"IF FEAR IS THE CORNERSTONE OF YOUR CHURCH, RUN."

Attending a church that teaches Christ-like love is important in building up a strong relationship with Jesus. So stay away from the places that teach:

"Do *this* or else!"

"Stop that *immediately* or you will lose your salvation!"

"If you don't *do* more for God, then He won't hear your prayers!"

That stuff is total crap. They have no clue who God really is.

Next up, I'd like to address the excuse of, "I don't need to go to church to be a Christian." I used this one for years. And sure, we don't *need* to go to church to be a Christian, but that attitude in itself goes against Christ's. So instead of saying, "I don't need church," let's turn it back around on ourselves. As I grew in my relationship with Jesus *without* church, I had no other option but to finally ask myself, *"Why am I really not going to church?"* My answer was this: *because I don't like church people.*

According to the Holy Spirit in me, that's not okay. God counseled me away from this incorrect mindset, and I immediately knew I needed to get back into church—if not for any other reason than to fight the devil. "Fight the devil?" you might ask. Yes, he was heavily influencing my feelings toward self-righteous do-gooders. I seriously disliked how I *felt* when I got around the people who snubbed their noses at me. I was letting *that* have a negative effect on my life. And all it really was, was bitterness. Again, the Holy Spirit of Christ does not approve of that and bitterness does not describe my perfect spirit at all (see Colossians 1:22, Galatians 5:22-23).

As a Christian I'm supposed to love everyone. Yet I had somehow fallen into the pit of seriously disliking Christians *as* a Christian. And what else is crazy, I developed an *over*-empathy for non-believers—especially those who got picked on by unloving Christians. Once again, this was not okay with God. I'm glad I can chuckle at it now, because that was really bad. To overcome this, I began to ask God, "Show me how to love religious people," and He has. This was one of my main reasonings for getting back in church.

Yes, we can pray at home—or anywhere—we can listen to Christian music and sing along while we're alone. We can even study our Bibles and watch a grace-filled teacher on TV or online, but church attendance is still important because certain people *at* that church might need our presence.

Hebrews 10:25 says we are "not to forsake the fellowship of one another"—and no, this is not a law telling Christians to "Go to church or else!" After all, the first church *building* wasn't even established until approximately 200 years after Christ lived. Instead, this verse is saying our gatherings can be a time of wonderful encouragement. If you read the verse right before this one, it explains the context, "And let us consider how we may spur one another on toward love and good deeds" (Hebrews 10:24).

Going to church also teaches us how to interact with each other as believers. Christian interaction is a very good thing! At church we learn corporately how to act (and react) toward non-believers, new Christians, weaker Christians, and even mature Christians. Which, if Christ is the center of the church, will always be *equally* with truth and love.

Another neat thing you will experience by attending a Christ-filled church is that you get to see and *feel* what it's like to have the Holy Spirit dwelling among so many people all at once! This cannot be described in words! It can only be felt in person and *cannot* be felt by yourself. No, we aren't "feeling chasers," but there is nothing wrong with feeling great feelings! The *corporate* feeling of the Holy Spirit is amazing! And I believe this feeling is so important because it's a preview of what heaven will be like, which is *all* believers enjoying the presence of God, together, forever!

GROWING PAINS HURT

Any type of growth in any real relationship—with *any* kind of true intimacy—will hurt you. Now, first of all, I want to make perfectly clear that I'm *not* talking about putting up with abuse or accepting unacceptable behavior as normal. As a matter of fact, the more you get to know Jesus and your true identity in Him, the more strength and confidence He gives you to be able to confront and combat such things. Once you understand your full value you stop putting up with so much crap, but you stop putting up with it in a loving, respectful, *stern* manner. This is possible! Boundaries are important for your well-being, and God knows that.

The Holy Spirit has given you the tools you need to be able to stand up for yourself in a proper manner that is natural to your perfect spirit (see Galatians 5:22-23). You have everything on the inside of you, you simply need to let it come *out* of you (see 2 Peter 1:3). This happens over time as you grow. Jesus wants you to confront your fears—not back down from them—but He wants you to do this in ways that match up with your heaven-ready identity. This will take some getting used to through practice as you develop the life you were created to live.

Your mind grows in healthy ways as you walk by *who* you are inside, so don't be hard on yourself during this process. Keep your *who* and your *do* separate. Soon enough you will see your growth flourish simply because of the trajectory of it. Just like an oak tree is an oak tree from the time it is a seed, it still takes years to grow *up and out* in order to become *big and strong*. However, from day *one* it was still an oak tree, so give your *own* growth time. Changes *will* happen organically, all around you, but this starts *within* you.

The growing pains in regard to our relationship with Christ is a pain in our *thinking*. This pain is a mind-renewal of how we're living and responding to the world when our lives and responses aren't matching up with our spirits. Now that we love Christ and have Him living in us, we naturally want to do things to make Him happy and proud because that's who we are. So the pain we feel comes from growing into our true identity—it's called growing pains for a reason! Our growth comes from us allowing Christ to prune off the stuff in our lives and minds that shouldn't be there. So don't be afraid of this pain! You are growing! Scream and cry if you have to, but keep growing and rest in Christ as you do!

As we get to know Jesus more and more each day through the Bible, prayer, His Spirit, and other graceful resources, we learn about *what* exactly He would and wouldn't approve of. We learn who we really are. These changes *will* hurt your unrenewed mindsets and fleshy desires. But just like the beginning of a brand new workout regimen that you know will eventually help you, the pain you experience is a very good thing because you are growing in strength! Also try to keep in mind that the pain is the very worst when we first start out. It does get easier as time goes on. We get *stronger* through resistance, not weaker.

"OUR GROWTH COMES FROM US ALLOWING CHRIST TO PRUNE OFF THE STUFF IN OUR LIVES AND MINDS THAT SHOULDN'T BE THERE."

Eventually, the difficult decisions that hurt us so badly in the beginning of allowing Christ to live through us are the very things that *enable* us enjoy our lives! This is why Paul said, "God's power is made perfect in our weakness" (see 2 Corinthians 12:9).

The devil will also notice your growth and he will begin to attack your mind, so be ready. Never believe his lies when he implies that God does *not* see your growth, nor does He care. Any size of growth is *very* impressive to God! He sees the effort you are putting into relying on Him and He is proud! So keep going!

Next, in order to be able to move further into your relationship with Jesus you must keep in the forefront of your mind that painful growth is *always* for the good. If we don't see painful growth as good then we will suffer the entire time it happens. Soon enough, we will becoming bitter, miserable, blameful, and weak—*as* a Christian. Eventually we'll blame God for our "sacrificial pain" and start to feel sorry for ourselves. Self-pity will then overtake us and we'll become completely useless—we'll become dormant branches. After that it's only a matter of time before we give up on allowing Jesus to live through us all together and we'll fall right back into living by what we are already dead to: *sin and stinking thinking*.

For this reason you *must* begin to look at your pain as a *good* thing. How can pain possibly be good? To answer that question look no further than the Cross of Christ. Hebrews 12:2 says, "For the joy set *before* him he *endured* the cross" (my emphasis added). What Jesus went through for us was extremely painful *while* He went through it! But it was joyful afterwards!

So by us continuing to look to *His* example as we allow God to help us grow into who *we* really are, we realize that our old mindsets are being *refined* by pain. He's not hurting us, He's helping us! Vines don't hurt their branches!

"YOU MUST BEGIN TO LOOK AT YOUR PAIN AS A *GOOD* THING. HOW CAN PAIN POSSIBLY BE GOOD? TO ANSWER THAT QUESTION LOOK NO FURTHER THAN THE CROSS OF CHRIST."

Thankfully, while we are in pain we are allowed to ask God to *stop* our pain, even Jesus did this (see Luke 22:42). At the same time, we should be honest about the *type* of pain we are feeling and not cover it up with fluff or fake, religious, rah-rah tag-lines, "Just carrying my cross! I guess I'll just keep suffering for Christ!" That is not what God wants you to do and it's also not healthy for your soul. Friend, please understand that you can go ahead and tell God, "Hey! This hurts! PLEASE CHANGE THIS! And please do it quickly!" You're allowed to talk to God about anything. You're allow to *say* anything to God about anything. But when you do, be sure to express to Him how much you love and trust Him no matter what He decides is best. This helps you grow even deeper into your loving trust with Him and that's what He wants the most.

Chapter 3

SUCCESS AND RELIGION CANNOT REPLACE CHRIST

"What good is it for someone to gain the whole world, yet forfeit their soul?" –*Jesus*

See MARK 8:36

"You who are trying to be justified by the Law have been alienated from Christ; you have fallen away from grace."

GALATIANS 5:4

TWO BIG LIES

During the times of our lives when we are ignoring God, living by the flesh and acting on our unrenewed mindsets, God keeps us safe for a specific reason: *He wants to use our poor choices and checkered past to help others who are going t through the same things.* My life is proof of this. Only by the grace of God am I writing this book. With the enormous amount of stupid choices I've made, I should probably be dead, in prison, or completely ruined—well, if the devil had his way with me anyway. Whether we realize it or not, the enemy is constantly trying to pull us away from our God-given destinies.

You see, as a human being, you are in one of two groups:

1. You are currently a Christian.
2. God is calling you to be one.

How do I know this? Because Jesus said, "When I am lifted up from earth, I will draw all people to myself" (see John 12:32). He was referring to what He'd be doing at the Cross. As of today, 2,000 years later, there has never been any other point in time in which God has had the ability to reach so many people all at once—so quickly and efficiently—*through* those who believe! (See Philippians 2:13). It's now our job to *act on* the promptings in which He is constantly nudging us with (see Mark 16:15).

Christ's return gets closer each day, so He wants us to use our experiences from when we continually abused His kindness to now *gracefully* pull people toward Him! The way we do this is by simply making ourselves available to God each day, through our actions and attitudes, and by showing others gentleness and respect (see 1 Peter 3:15).

Since I've been to the bottom of the barrel—actually, so far *under* the barrel I couldn't even dig any deeper—I can now help those who are currently struggling with the same things. I know what it's like to live a frustrating, blameful, over-worked life. I know what it feels like to be addicted and full of self-pity, while surrounded by people who don't appreciate you but instead use you for all you've got.

So now I want to use my gifts and past to help those who are battling poverty, abuse, loneliness, abandonment, divorce, adultery, boundary confusion, and codependency. Why? Because I've been there. But I also want to help people who are struggling with two very overlooked issues which can cause many problems in their lives: *success and religion.*

"SINCE I'VE BEEN TO THE BOTTOM OF THE BARREL— ACTUALLY, SO FAR UNDER THE BARREL THAT I COULDN'T EVEN DIG ANY DEEPER—I CAN NOW HELP THOSE WHO ARE CURRENTLY STRUGGLING WITH THE SAME THINGS."

These are two big lies used by the devil to disrupt your enjoyment of simply being a branch connected to the vine, who is Christ. He wants you to think being successful financially as well as becoming uber-legalistic will *enhance* your relationship with Jesus. They won't. Instead, both can *replace* intimacy with Him. Many people really do struggle with succeeding financially, as strange as that sounds. You might be thinking, "I'd like to struggle that way!" but I'm here to tell you, when money is no longer a problem, that in itself can *become* the problem if you begin to think you no longer need God's guidance.

It's the same with religion. Maybe this is the first book you've ever read about God, and my style of ministering clicks well with your soul. Great! I feel honored! However, your growth in Christ will take you through many different teachers and eventually to church—more than likely anyway. So if you've not had to deal with anything "churchy" just yet, make no mistake you will. With that being said, I want to help you be aware of a trap waiting for you which has been personally set by Satan himself *at* church.

Sounds bad, I know, but just because you walk through the church doors that doesn't mean the devil and his crew stay outside. He is going to try to get you to think your identity is *in* that building, and *in* the opinion of those people. It's not. Yes, you should respect both and consider the guidance of leaders. However, finding your identity in religion or church can absolutely ruin your relationship with Christ. Religion causes you to desperately seek out your pastor's or priest's approval in all things. Eventually, we can even shipwreck our *close* relationship with Jesus because we are so driven to impress this person who is up on stage each week.

I'm not saying you'll become unsaved by putting your pastor or priest on a pedestal, that's impossible (see 2 Timothy 2:13, Hebrews 7:25, John 10:28). But you *can* muffle the Holy Spirit's leadership by looking to a man or woman *above* God (Ephesians 4:30). For some, this will be hard to hear, but I'll say it anyway: *your pastor or priest is not always right, and they are no more holy than a prostitute who just got saved today.* This is why we must keep our *spiritual* identity in perspective at all times by realizing we are all of equal value to our Creator and we all get the same reward *now* and in the end: *Christ in us, forever* (see Galatians 3:28, Colossians 1:27, 3:11, Matthew 20:1-16).

"I WANT TO HELP YOU BE AWARE OF A TRAP WAITING FOR YOU WHICH HAS BEEN PERSONALLY SET BY SATAN HIMSELF *AT* CHURCH."

Friend, God didn't deliver you out of your past just so that you can become a slave to church. He didn't guide you out of the fire for you to stay under the guilt and condemnation of legalistic people who simply want to use you. No way. Instead, God wants to use both church *and* religious people to develop your perseverance, maturity, and reliance on Him (see James 1:2-4).

So remember that your relationship with Jesus is based on *His* finished work at the Cross and by understanding that you have a brand new *perfect* spirit which is intertwined with Him for good—no matter where your physical body is at on this planet. *You* are the church because God has made His home *in* you! (See Romans 6:6, Colossians 3:3, Galatians 2:20, 1 Corinthians 6:19).

I don't want to be misunderstood, please know that *church* is not the problem. Church can be a very good thing! What I'm referring to is a works-based, quasi-grace clique. You know, the people who believe you have to work your way to heaven by what you do and don't do? Those who push the lie that you can actually *lose* your spiritual rebirth by not living up to *their* standards? I'm talking about the arrogant folk who represent the *real* prodigal son, the "good one" who stayed home with the father and behaved? This group absolutely *refuses* to apply Christ's love to anyone unless they do their religious duties *just* like them. You may or may not have had any dealings just yet with such people, but more than likely you will.

These Christians will attempt to make you feel *so* bad, that you may even want to end your own life. After all, you can't *possibly* live up to their standards, no matter what you do. They'll try to make you feel like a beat dog. They want you to think there is nothing good about yourself. They've removed grace from the gospel, "Because it gives you a license to sin!" They are cold, stiff, sharp and if you don't do what they say or fall in line behind them, you will become excommunicated from their home Bible study small groups.

"THEY'LL TRY TO MAKE YOU FEEL LIKE A BEAT DOG. THEY WANT YOU TO THINK THERE IS NOTHING GOOD ABOUT YOURSELF."

Then they'll give up on you completely, "Because it's biblical," while labeling you as "unrepentant." Next, they will ask you to flat out leave their church or to get "plugged in" somewhere else so they no longer have to deal with someone such as yourself. Then they'll judge you harshly as one of the main subjects of their unloving, stiff sermons, in front of their congregations, all the while using *you* as an example of who *not* to be like.

Lastly, they'll white-wash their disgusting treatment of you by calling it "discernment." *This* is the religion I'm referring to. It can ruin your life.

What's most sad is this charade has nothing to do with *your* relationship with Jesus, it's a distraction. So please be aware of that.

This stuff is simply a spike-strip thrown down in the middle of the path of your God-given destiny meant to blow out the tires on your joy! Please begin to recognize that the devil is conducting this whole thing *through* religious people. Jesus does *not* see you like they do! He loves you unconditionally and sees your full potential.

Now let's talk about money. In regard to success—and I say this with sincere humbleness—I've experienced it. From a very young age, I've experienced extreme success in business. My success however does not define who I am. Oh I *thought* it did! But it does not! Jesus taught me that even if I'm broke, I'm still rich because of my faith in Him.

"I LEARNED AT A VERY YOUNG AGE TO NOT BE JEALOUS OF SUCCESSFUL PEOPLE, BUT INSTEAD, JUST WORK HARDER THAN THEM."

One very important thing I've learned about being successful in my career is that jealousy would always *hinder* my success. It wasn't until I started to truly be happy for others that my own career really took off. This is why you should never be jealous of what other people have if you aren't willing to do the same things they did to get it. I learned in my teenage years to not be jealous of successful people, but instead, just work harder than them. Working hard for your salvation does nothing, but in business, the opposite applies.

Attaining your career goals, although very important, this does *not* produce the fulfillment you think it will. It's a mirage. Once you finally get there, it's empty. For me, as a weak Christian, all financial success really did was replace my complete dependance on God with money and stuff.

There is nothing wrong with having money, at all. Money is a great tool given to us by God and if it's applied properly to your life it can be used to live comfortably, to help others, and most importantly, to spread the gospel. Remember, it's okay to have money, but it's not okay to let money have you.

When and if God blesses you with financial success, if you're not careful it will simply replace your intimacy with Him. Money can even go to your head, causing you to have a poor attitude of, "I have money. I don't need anything else, or anyone else. So back off!" When this happens, the faster you recognize the devil's blindfold on you, the faster God can get you back on track, by removing it. How? Through a very difficult step: *humbling yourself*. You must humble yourself despite the fact that you don't *need* Him to bless you financially any longer. Y Your begging is over, He's gotten you out of the hole.

The *love* of being successful is a huge distraction sent to us from hell. In my lifetime, the most enticing replacement for Christ's guidance has always been success. Before my fall, my story included not just pride, but also greed. I soon figured out that growing in a close relationship with Jesus removes both incorrect mindsets.

SUCCESS

Isn't it amazing how we are so quick to blame God for everything bad that happens in our lives, but when we succeed we never want to give Him any credit? That was me. Now, I need to say this without sounding arrogant, so please don't think that is my goal: *I've been extremely successful in my line of business*. I know what it's like to have your financial dreams come true through hard work, determination, and doing things others won't do. *However*, I also know what it's like to live on food stamps just to be able to feed your family. I've been *without* money for most of my life, and I've not inherited a dime from anyone.

So although *now*, at the age of 34, I'm living a comfortable life, used to be, that was far from reality. I had debts I couldn't pay which seriously ticked people off. I even had to move into my father-in-law's basement for a time, just to be able to make it through the year. I strained and struggled every day, begging God to help me get on my feet. I would even work out deals with Him, "Okay God, I'll do *this*, if you do *that*." At the time, I didn't realize God doesn't work that way. Knowing what I now know I have a feeling He just chuckled at me, "Ha! No you won't. But I'll bless you anyway, Matthew. Only because I love you."

My life hasn't always been like it currently is. People see the fruit of my labor but they have no idea what I had to go through to grow it. For many years, I had to clip Burger King coupons and count change from the cup-holder just so that I can get a Whopper with cheese once a week, as a special treat. I've dealt with *extreme* financial hardships, both as a child and as an adult. So I can talk about that lifestyle as well, in very great detail.

"I WOULD EVEN WORK OUT DEALS WITH HIM, 'OKAY GOD, I'LL DO THIS, IF YOU DO THAT.' AT THE TIME I DIDN'T REALIZE GOD DOESN'T WORK THAT WAY."

But as for being successful in business, I know what it feels like to be at the pinnacle of your industry! I know *exactly* what it takes to be a leader in your field! I've experienced nearly everything you could possibly think of *just* to be able to get to the point of saying, "Yes, my company is successful." And to be perfectly honest with you, of course it's nice to not have to worry about checking on gas prices each day, but at the end of the day, I'd have to say that being successful in business *overall* is a thankless endeavor which is extremely stressful, difficult, and scary. It takes a mind-blowing amount of time, energy, and effort, just to be able to say, "Yep, I got stuff."

Before I got to this point, I used to idolize the people who had nice cars or above-average homes, those who went on trips, or didn't worry about the extras—I wanted to be like them. Back in my greedy days, I looked up to the people who had "made it," not yet realizing *that* means nothing to God without Christ as your leader. God has taught me that pretty much anyone can make money—both legally and illegally—but not everyone is willing to make God, who provides all things, of any importance in their lives.

The Bible says, "It is God who gives us the ability to acquire wealth" (see Deuteronomy 8:18). So when we ignore Him while He is blessing us financially, we are simply taking credit for something we didn't completely do on our own. God's desire is for our attention to be brought to Him through everything we do! This includes building a business or advancing in our careers.

But back when I was ignoring the Holy Spirit's guidance, I had made Him out to be just a little pet I kept in my pocket. I'd let Him peek out every once in a while as I fed Him an M&M while patting Him on the head. Yes, I knew He was real, but I hardly paid Him any notice. Because of my fleshy desire to earn more—along with my incorrect mindset of *"Money makes a man"*—in my mind I viewed God as small, mean, and constantly waiting for me to mess up. I had no trust in Him and no confidence either. Even though He lived in me, I hardly knew Him, by my own choice. Sure, if you asked me, I was saved, "But whatever! Let's just make some money!" was how I thought.

Once God finally helped me back on my feet, I gave Him very little honor or acknowledgment. Instead, I developed even *more* wants, and even *more* grief. The lazy people who used me all along got worse, and the guilt trips from those who knew I now had money—"So give me some of it"—flooded my life. Soon enough, I became frustrated and driven to make even more. Success had gone to my head, my focus in life was way off, and I had become a slave to the opinion of people. Thankfully, by the grace of God, He began to help redirect my reliance for joy *back* onto Him.

"THE LAZY PEOPLE WHO USED ME ALL ALONG, GOT WORSE. AND THE GUILT TRIPS FROM THOSE WHO KNEW I NOW HAD MONEY—'SO GIVE ME SOME OF IT'—FLOODED MY LIFE."

I'm not saying it's bad to have money. What I'm saying is that it's bad to let money have *you*. It's good to have financial goals and you should! However, *attaining* those goals does not mean that everything in your life will simply fall into place. Once you "make it" all of the hard work isn't over—not even close. So if you think you'll only be happy and content *after* you climb the corporate ladder, open up multiple locations, get that big raise or find your dream job, I'm not here to burst your bubble but that will not happen.

If someone tells you that your life will finally be complete only after you make money, or that all of your dreams will come true once you've established yourself financially, that person is lying to you. Either because they've not attained those goals themselves, or they have, but they are still in denial about the truth.

The *honest* truth is even when you *do* secure your career goals, that success in itself *can't* replace a close relationship with God. It's absolutely impossible. The God-shaped hole in your soul can only be filled up perfectly by enjoying a relationship with Jesus. Yeah, we can try, and try, and *try* to shove all types of things in there, including money, but nothing fits just right except for a moment by moment walk with Christ. As I mentioned in the beginning of this book, God made us like this on purpose because He wants the longing in our souls to only be satisfied by Him.

This is one of the main reasons why we should never be jealous of people who are well-off financially. First of all, because jealousy doesn't match up with our true identity, but secondly, we must remember that just because someone has money that doesn't mean they are any more important to God or any *less* important, either. We are all the same in the eyes of

God, we are *individually* loved children. Our faith in Jesus Christ *completes* this love and then allows us to enjoy it.

It doesn't matter to God how *much* money we have or how *little* money we have, He cares about what *money* will do to our lives. And just because someone does have money, that doesn't mean their life is any easier, especially if they don't have a relationship with Jesus. Money, or lack thereof, cannot replace our craving to enjoy Jesus. We all thirst for knowing Him more and more, no matter if we are a billionaire or on welfare.

"WE ALL THIRST FOR KNOWING HIM MORE AND MORE, NO MATTER IF WE ARE A BILLIONAIRE OR ON WELFARE."

When you become successful you don't realize it's just the beginning of many *other* problems which will arise. The devil starts to throw major issues into the mix, most of which you never thought could possibly happen *after* you didn't have to worry about money. H Here is a huge facade that financially comfortable people put on: *"My life looks happy from the outside, because my bank account is in the black."* However, that's not always the case.

Being successful in your career without Jesus as your leader brings on a whole new list of hidden problems that you didn't even know existed. These problems only pop up and rear their ugly heads after you start to buy nice things, eat expensive meals, take fancy trips, and splurge on the leather-trimmed packages. All of these things in themselves are *not* the problem at all. Really, money isn't even the issue here. The main problem is when God decides to bless us with money and we quickly replace the Holy Spirit as our Counselor with Benjamin Franklin. We also make dollar signs and the stuff we have as the main source of our identity. *That's* the problem. *That's* what God does not approve of. It's not the *having* of money God hates, it's the *letting money have you* that He can't stand. Never feel guilty about making money, but always beware of money making you.

As for my upbringing, my success had nothing to do with coming from a healthy home. I didn't have the *Leave it to Beaver* family. I know what it feels like to be a little kid ripped away from both parents and thrown into foster homes. I've experienced the deep pain of being separated from my siblings while being abused by employees of the State. I know what it's like to cry yourself to sleep each night while curled up on the bottom bunk of a room *filled* with bunk-beds, surrounded by strange kids who are also crying—just not as quietly—all the while begging God, "Please just get me out of here so I can get back to my family."

As a little boy, I honestly thought it was that easy. I thought that if I just prayed long enough and good enough, the doors would open up and I could somehow walk out without anyone noticing. I could then just go find my family, get us all back together, and things would be normal and happy again. Even now, thinking back on those days I hurt for the kid-version of me. I wish I could go back in time and hug him, comfort him, and tell him that everything works out wonderfully. He was a sad little boy who endured a lot. He had to deal with tons of things that no child should *ever* have to deal with. But even then, God was already hard at work in my life. He was making sure that everything was coming together for my *eventual* benefit, but more importantly, for His glory.

This sounds really strange, but if you asked me, "Do you regret your childhood?" I would say, "No, I don't." I don't regret God allowing those things to happen to me because even then He was *already* giving me the grace I needed to be able make it through anything. This amazing thing called *grace* I would learn to rely on for the rest of my life—but I wouldn't begin to fully enjoy it until my thirties.

Next, I'd like to tell you about my life in business. Unlike our relationship with God, hard work is the determining factor to achieve the best results. As an entrepreneur, I understand what starting from scratch is like. I can empathize with those who are fearful and broke, yet courageous and excited! I know how demeaning it can feel to borrow gas money from your grandma, just to have enough fuel to be able to go door to door, trying to sell security systems. For nearly 15 years, the home security industry has been my livelihood. In order to build *up* my company, beginning at the age of nineteen, I would go door to door for eight to ten hours per day. I soon figured out the very *key* to success in sales: *Try. Never stop trying.*

Again, this is the opposite of what the gospel requires, but all you really have to do to be successful is keep on keeping on. If one thing works—great! Keep moving in that direction! If it doesn't, then take a step back and move in a different direction. Don't *do* that again, or don't *say* that again. Remember, *you* are the only one who is responsible for giving yourself a chance, nobody else is!

If you're in sales, and you'll begin to form this mindset, the many excuses that the less-successful people have will not be a part of your vocabulary. Also, be sure to remove quickly the thoughts that tell you, "Nobody wants this," or "Everyone tells me *no*," and worst of all, *never* say, "I'm no good at this." These things are not true!

There are no principles in the gospel because that would require a law. But for sales, understanding the principle of, "Work as if everything depends on me. Pray as if everything depends on God" will create success for you! Always keep a positive, open mind, no matter *what* you face or *who* you face! You *will* win, somehow, someway!

Keep doing what you *can* do, keep controlling what you *can* control—and do it with enthusiasm! Never worry about what you have no control over! If you do, then you will become discouraged and negative. That's exactly what the devil wants from you. He's not here to just ruin your spiritual life but also your financial life!

"AS LONG AS YOU DON'T QUIT, YOU CAN NEVER REALLY FAIL."

As long as you don't quit, you can never really fail. And even when you *do* fail, God will use your defeats as lessons for the next chapter in your career. On the days when I gave it my best shot and it still didn't produce anything, I always came back to try again the next morning. Resiliency was something I learned at a young age. I always woke up early, took my shower, ate some breakfast, and put on a button-up shirt and nice pants. I'd have my entire day planned out. From 8:00 am to 6:00 pm, or until I got at least two sales, I would not stop going door to door.

I *knew*, deep inside, the faster I got people to tell me "No," the faster I would be able to find someone who would tell me "Yes." In door to door sales, you have an unlimited amount of appointments each day, all day long! It's just that the people you have appointments with don't know you've got them penciled-in.

Cold-calling (I never called it that because those words seemed negative, but that's what it was) petrified me to the core—but only at first. Next to public speaking and spiders, door to door sales ranks in the top ten fears of human beings. Most people run for the hills when this duty is brought up during job interviews. But as a young man, what made my new job even *more* scary was the fact that I had no idea what I was doing, or much about what I was selling. Nobody trained me. That didn't stop me though. I was determined to figure this out! In my soul I *knew* that I had the keys to the vehicle of what would now drive my career. However, it was still *my* responsibility to drive it effectively and efficiently. So each and every day, I always forced myself through the fear of knocking on my very first door.

Some days I would pull up to a house literally shaking with my heart racing, my shirt would be soaked with sweat, all the while I was trying to pump myself up to just get out of the dang car. Sometimes I'd back out the driveway, and ride around the neighborhood for five or ten minutes, mad at myself for being afraid. Then I'd go back and *force* myself out of the car, still full of fear, walk up, and then knock on my first door.

The beauty of this method of *pushing through my fears* resulted in me realizing my fears were stupid. They were. After all, what's the worst that could happen? In my mind it was probably getting cursed out and the door slammed in my face, but even still, so what. *"As long as they do it quickly, I won't take it personal,"* was the mindset I had.

-⊛⊛⊛-

"BUSINESS OWNERSHIP IS NOT FOR THE WEARY, FOR THE BLAMERS, OR FOR THE EXCUSE-GIVERS. AT THE END OF THE DAY, YOU ARE RESPONSIBLE FOR EVERYTHING."

-⊛⊛⊛-

The reality was most people were kind. As I look back now, I could see that God was teaching me how to push through my fears by being courageous. In turn, He was blessing me financially on a level unlike I could have ever planned or imagined. It was insane. Sometimes I would be on my drive home and I would breakdown in tears of gratefulness.

However, business ownership is not for the weary, for the blamers, or for the excuse-givers. At the end of the day, *you* are responsible for everything. Owning your own company takes a ton self-discipline, a ridiculous amount dedication, and tremendous sacrifice of your personal time. But when you stick it out and press forward, and you finally *do* have success, you have to learn how to *not* let it go to your head—or worse, form your identity. You must remember that money does not define you, God does.

Ultimately, my goal of achieving financial freedom was so my family and I could enjoy life more, so I could help others, and so I could spread the gospel with my earnings. It worked! My company, Alarm Security, is now one of the most trusted names in home and business security in the entire State of Missouri! God did that *for* me, *through* me!

RELIGION

Jesus didn't come to earth to start a religion, He came to earth to start a relationship—a personal one, individually, with each of us. *Religion* is man's way of twisting, and making extremely difficult, what Christ died to make so easy. There are many different Christian denominations which display man's self-centeredness. However, Jesus didn't have a denomination. In my mind, I can hear one of the early Christians who broke off from the others, say, "I want to do this *my* way, and with *my* rules." Jesus, on the other hand, simply wanted us all to form one group: *the Church* (see 1 Corinthians 12:12, 12:27, Romans 12:5, Galatians 3:28).

The pride of man caused this idea to be destroyed soon after Jesus ascended. In turn, denominations were formed. Denomination is just another word for *division*. For me, I don't have one. I'm a Christian and that's it. I don't *need* a label on it. I love Jesus, I have a new spirit, I'm excited about God, and now I want to help other people find and enjoy the same thing. I believe this should be our goal as Christians. Instead of nitpicking rules, regulations, and styles, I think we should love each other as Christ loves us. We can accomplish this feat by letting Jesus live *through us*, with grace. The Holy Spirit will guide us to love and respect everyone, whether we believe exactly like them or not. We don't have to agree with someone's doctrine in order to be able to think of them with love and goodness.

We're not God. We don't have a heaven or hell to throw anyone into, so *our* job is to simply do our very best to get this good news out there, and to do it with grace. I've prayed for, hand in hand, and had long conversations with atheists, Muslims, Satanists, and even agnostics. I have nothing against anyone or any religion. I am simply *for* the truth of the gospel. We all have free access to this gift from God by grace through faith in Jesus as our Savior. Period. No exceptions.

"INSTEAD OF NITPICKING RULES, REGULATIONS, AND STYLES, I THINK WE SHOULD LOVE EACH OTHER AS CHRIST LOVES US."

If someone's method of spreading the gospel goes against the grace of God, then I'm against their method. Without grace, none of us would stand a chance. We must remember that it's not about our style of Christianity that matters to God. Instead, it's about His grace which is handed out to *each* style, through Christ, undeservedly.

For example, in the Book of Acts, the disciples speak in tongues—great! I wouldn't mind to speak in tongues either, however, it's never happened to me so I'm not going to force it. There is no law in speaking in tongues—how foolish. But I've heard some preachers say that if you *don't* speak in tongues then you don't r really have the Holy Spirit in you. What a load of crap! Because yes I do! Paul said that if you belong to Christ, then you *do* have His Spirit in you (see Romans 8:9). Chanting, "Daddy-shoulda-bought-a-Honda," doesn't magically cause God to infuse Himself with your spirit.

That "second blessing" garbage does nothing but create fear and anxiety for a believer. We don't *need* a second blessing, as if our first blessing wasn't enough. Instead, we've *been blessed* (past tense) with every spiritual blessing in Christ (see Ephesians 1:3). Once again, this is *religion*, denominations, works, effort, hierarchies, and legalism. That's what I'm against. I'm against self-righteous, graceless, controlling, manipulating, pretzel-twisting of the gospel, religion.

"IF YOU REALLY KNEW JESUS AND HOW HE WORKS, YOU WOULDN'T BE ABLE TO NOT LOVE HIM!"

Religion removes the need for *just* Jesus. It's a "Jesus-plus" relationship, which is no real relationship at all. Religion is *our* version of God's truth which has brought so much *untruth* into the world. Religion is what killed Jesus. Religion has given Jesus a bad name. If you really knew Jesus and how He works, you wouldn't be able to *not* love Him! But religion has made Him nearly unloveable! Religion is our misrepresentation of Christ, and *that* is what makes people not want anything to do with Him.

I had a conversation the other day with someone and they were trying to pin a denomination on me. They just could *not* understand that I don't have one.

"But, you *have* to have one."

"No I don't."

"Yeah, you do."

This person had been so religiously brain-washed that they couldn't comprehend that I don't have a denomination. I'm a Christian, that's it! As for my theology? It's simple: Jesus Christ died for me because He loves me, and because I needed Him to. I believe He is the Savior of my sin problem. My life is now Christ's life, and I have a brand new spirit which is connected to Jesus for good. His death on the Cross removed all of my sin once and for all by killing off my old spirit and giving me a heaven-ready spirit.

No denomination needed. No religion needed. Just Jesus. Just a new spirit.

If someone reading this has a religious spirit that normally pesters them, I'm sure it's all riled up. So I'll tell you this: if I *could* achieve more from God by doing things a different way, I would! But I can't! Neither can you! Neither can anyone! This is why grace was such a wonderful idea.

Now to be honest with you, I used to be a complete slave to religion. Just like so many other frustrated Christians, I thought that I had to *act* a certain way, *walk* a certain way, *talk* a certain way, *praise God* a certain way, and *dress* a certain way—wrong! And if others didn't do it just like me then "They just ain't Christian!" It was so silly!

Maybe you've had to deal people who use the name of Christ to control you instead of love you. Maybe someone has shamed you and guilted you incessantly, rather than try to guide you and teach you *lovingly*. Maybe they've said that if you ever miss church, or hang out with people who make poor choices, *you* will be in jeopardy of going to hell. "Backslider!" they call you. Do you know anyone like this? Have you personally experienced such terrible treatment? Because of *their* actions you think, "If this is how God really is, then I don't want anything to do with Him." My friend, THAT'S NOT GOD! That's *them*!

"BECAUSE OF THEIR ACTIONS, YOU THINK, 'IF THIS IS HOW GOD REALLY IS, THEN I DON'T WANT ANYTHING TO DO WITH HIM.'"

I know about this *very* well, as I have experienced it greatly! The devil wanted me to hate these people, and the sin of my flesh did, with all its might! Then one day, God opened up my eyes as to what was really going on. Religion. Religion is what was going on. He showed me that their actions had nothing to do with Jesus. Once I learned this, everything changed. Even though it was like eating glass at first—because of my unrenewed mindsets—I began to *genuinely* love religious people. Yes, I'm still a work in progress, but oh my *goodness* I'm *so* much better than I used to be!

Let me ask you, do you think that all Christians are harsh and extremely judgmental? Every single one of them? Do you believe they are all just a bunch of terrible people who dislike you? Do you have the mindset of, "Church people rub me the wrong way"? Well I did too, and that is not where God wants us to stay. The devil sure does, but God doesn't.

Growing up, I was blessed with an angel of a grandmother who raised me. She prayed for me constantly, cared for me endlessly, and loved me deeply—as if I were her own son. But the best thing about Grandma was that she *showed* me Jesus. My dad's mom, her name is Mae Lorene McMillen, "Lorene" to some, but "Grandma" or "Granny Mac" to most, she is very special. Grandma is special on a level unlike you can possibly understand without personally knowing her. God simply does *not* make them like her anymore. The mold was broken in heaven after she was born.

Even at 86 years old, she is *still* doing h her very best to get the word out for Jesus. This lady is absolutely the best thing that ever happened to me, as well as to thousands of other people. I can only imagine what it will be like when she goes to heaven. For us, we'll have to rent a stadium instead of using a funeral home just to be able to fit in everyone who loved her. God blessed me before I was even born by Him letting me call this woman *Grandma*. She personifies Christ almost flawlessly. She showed me who Jesus really is. How did she do this? With one word: *love*. She exudes the most sincere, deep, unconditional form of love for absolutely everybody. I've never seen anything like it.

"THE BEST THING ABOUT GRANDMA WAS THAT SHE SHOWED ME JESUS."

However, on the other side of my family, my mom's dad, he did the very *opposite* for me of what my grandma did. He showed me who Christ was *not*. When it came to how Christians were supposed to treat people and love others—when it came to *religion*—this man was a monster. He did more false advertising for Jesus than almost anyone I've ever known, mainly because of the extreme hurt, fear, and anxiety he caused me as a boy. But also because he was an actual preacher—a preacher who spat out hell, fire, and damnation all over the place. He was meaner than a wet hornet. That's why nobody went to his church except for my step-grandma and their kids. This was the man who jacked up my mom's childhood too.

He caused ridiculous amounts of unnecessary, confidence-destroying, Bible-twisting problems galore. Had I kept in my mind what I thought about God, through what he attempted to build up in my head, who knows where I'd be today. I WOULD HATE GOD. I would also hate every single Christian *and* Christianity.

Nowadays he's a brittle old man and I've forgiven him. However, I still need to say that no kid should *ever* have t to deal with the mental and physical abuse that he put us through—*specifically* from someone who is supposed to be loving you, protecting you, and nurturing you—your own grandfather. It took me years to forgive this person, much less call him "Grandpa."

Jesus said that a tree is known by its fruit (see Luke 6:44), and this man's fruit was dead, maggot-filled, and rotten. He *completely* misrepresented Jesus, *as* a preacher. He is the most ornery man I've ever known. Even to this day, I can't think of anyone more cantankerous. But to top it off, he claimed to be an actual *teacher* of God's Word, proving to me that just because you stand in a pulpit, that doesn't mean you stand for Christ—or that Christ stands behind you.

So when it comes to having the deep-down notion of either wanting to *hate* God—because of a hateful preacher—or being completely *petrified* of Him—because someone instilled in you tremendous fear—my friend, I know how you feel. I was there too, and it's no place to stay. That is *far* from what Jesus desires for you. He wants you to have peace.

One more very important thing He has taught me about religion is this: *I can't base my faith on anyone else's actions or attitudes.* Instead, I have to love and forgive them just as Christ did for *me* because that's who I really am—I'm forgiven. I also have to stay focused on who *Jesus* is, rather than on the words and actions of those who claim to be vouching for Him. His Holy Spirit will actually use these types of people to teach you who He's *not*, if you let Him! He is not about religion! He is about relationship!

Chapter 4

STOP IGNORING GOD. ANSWER YOUR CALLING. UNLOCK YOUR DESTINY.

"For God's gifts and his call are irrevocable."

See ROMANS 11:29

I REALLY WANT WHAT GOD WANTS?

Here is a Facebook post I once wrote:

> Christian, God doesn't see you as a person who lives by the flesh and old stinking thinking. His view of you is completely different than anything you've ever known. He sees you as someone who wants what *He* wants—because you actually do!

> You may *think* you know yourself well, but your Creator knows you much better! From the very moment you first believed in Jesus' forgiveness, your old spirit died with Christ in the supernatural realm. You were then buried and resurrected as a *new* spirit! (See Romans 6:6, 2 Corinthians 5:17, Galatians 2:20).

You *are* a spirit, you *have* a soul, and you *live* in a body. You are now intermingled with God's own Spirit forever while still in this temporary physical vessel! (See Colossians 3:3, 1 Corinthians 6:19, Romans 8:9, John 14:23, Revelation 3:20). This is why *as a Christian* you actually have the exact same desires as God! You want what He wants! Why do you think that *now* when you sin, it never feels right? It's because sin will never match up with your perfect spiritual identity. Further, once you've received your new spirit, God places some very special things inside of you—He does this *on* purpose and *for* a purpose—an eternal purpose!

Yes, of course, you can try to cover them up or ignore them, but those gifts and that calling He's placed inside of you are irrevocable (see Romans 11:29). Irrevocable means you *can't* make them go away! Irrevocable means no returns, refunds, or exchanges! THEY ARE YOURS! You can pay them no mind for your entire life, but they will still be there the whole time you're alive.

The key to tapping into your gifts and calling is so easy: *be yourself*. "What? That's it? Matt, how can that be true when I'm a sinner?" you might say. My friend, you are not a sinner—you *were* a sinner, but now you are a holy, blameless saint *in* your spirit! Your spirit is the real you! (See Colossians 1:22). So all you have to do is be you!

If you *don't* do this, then the God-given stuff on the inside of you—the things He wants to use to alter history and heaven—will stay locked away *inside* of you.

But if you will finally open up this amazing treasure-chest on the inside of your spirit *with* Jesus, spectacular things will happen in your life! Astounding accomplishments will follow you everywhere you go! God will work *through* you *with* you, to do big things! Let's goooooooooooo!

...After reading that post you can see that I'm highly excited about who we are as God's kids. For me, I received my new, heaven-ready spirit as a boy, but I muffled my spirit as well as God's Spirit for most of my life. I want to help you *not* make that same mistake.

Part of my gifts and calling is for me to get *you* excited about your new self's capabilities—I want to encourage you. An element of my God-given purpose is my writings. I'm simply acting on a never-ending nudge from the Holy Spirit within. Trust me when I say this is a *lot* of work. My full-time job of running a security company takes up most of my time, but this is still very important to me—and I enjoy it.

I'm a very busy person. Absolutely no part of my day is wasted if I can help it. I used to think something was wrong with me because of my in-ability to just sit on the couch. However, God has taught me that He wired me this way for a reason and as long as I am keeping things in balance, I can fully enjoy my life with myself.

I know God has given me a gift of writing. I can communicate very well with written and spoken words. But the thought of me actually committing myself to writing a book was something I ignored for a long time—I went *away* from this calling. But like Jonah being spit up by the whale and God telling him, "Now go do what I told you to do in the first place" (see Jonah 3), I decided to finally commit myself to *using* my gifts for God. I'm glad I did because I really like this!

As for anyone who is a new creation in Christ, just because we ignore God's promptings that doesn't mean the urges will go away. The Holy Spirit is constantly speaking to our souls, saying, "C'mon, this way." We are His agents! We are His ambassadors! We represent God in this foreign land! (See 2 Corinthians 5:20). Our Creator's system works *through* people (see Philippians 2:13), so when we ignore the Holy Spirit and *don't* act, then it's not just us who misses out on enjoying our calling, but also count-less amounts of others as well.

⌘

"WHEN WE IGNORE THE HOLY SPIRIT AND DON'T ACT, THEN IT'S NOT JUST US WHO MISSES OUT ON ENJOYING OUR CALLING, BUT ALSO COUNTLESS AMOUNTS OF OTHERS AS WELL."

⌘

The ink on the blueprint of enjoying our full potential is this: *we must act!* The longer we wait to act, the longer we will have to wait to revel in who we really are! God wants us to step *through* our fears and discomforts without hesitation! This is called courage! We learn to trust Him as we move forward in action *through* courage *despite* our fear!

Like me writing this book, there is something about *your* life that God wants you to begin to act on—something that will propel you much higher in your level of heavenly use. Now please don't get me wrong. This has nothing to do with your salvation or with "storing up" heavenly rewards. Our salvation is secure in Christ no matter what we do or don't do because Jesus will never die again (see Hebrews 7:25). As for rewards, Christ *in us* right now is our *real* reward! (See Colossians 1:27, Matthew 20:1-16).

We are secure and complete right now! But when we *act on* who we really are in spirit, we can change this entire world for the better! You don't *have* to be doing mission work in the Congo, and you don't *have* to be a church planter in Chicago. You don't *have* to be a pastor or a secretary at church. All you have to do each day is wake up and say, "God, I love you, and I'm available to you." That's it! There is no pressure on you whatsoever!

The moment you start to feel pressure is the moment you know God isn't involved in *those* particular attitudes and actions—so recenter. Remember, we are simply *branches* and He is the vine (see John 15:5). Vines never pressure branches into doing anything. Instead, the branches just *be* themselves as they get all they are *from* the vine. We never have to worry about what happens when we decide to make ourselves available to God! *He* takes care of us! It's a beautiful thing!

God has been preparing us our entire lives for *this* moment in time. All of our past hurts, disappointments, struggles, addictions, successes, and failures, those things are now being used *for* our purpose. That purpose is to help others see Christ's love for them more clearly. From our past experiences with extremely loving Christians, to that with extremely unloving, cold, legalistic Christians—God is using it! From our childhoods to our parenting, to our marriages, our jobs, and schooling—God is currently using all things together for good! (See Romans 8:28). *All* of these things, circumstances, and people, God has allowed into our lives (*allowed*, not caused) so that we can help others with the very same issues! None of it was in vain!

My friend, God wants to use every single one of your life experiences *for* a greater good. He wants to use all of the stuff you've been through, to not only help you find joy and strength, but also to help others do the same. You might have even battled cancer—He wants to use that too! God plans on taking that mess of yours and making a beautiful message out of it! He wants to use your story to stock the halls of heaven full of souls! This is why absolutely *nothing* you've gone through has been pointless! No tear has gone unnoticed! No injustice ignored! No heartache or pain not felt by God Himself! IT WAS FOR YOUR PURPOSE!

"WE NEVER HAVE TO WORRY ABOUT WHAT HAPPENS WHEN WE DECIDE TO MAKE OURSELVES AVAILABLE TO GOD! HE TAKES CARE OF US! IT'S A BEAUTIFUL THING!"

And now He wants to use all of it for Him. He want to use it to bring attention to Jesus Christ, but you have to let Him. You have to stop ignoring Him and start listening. You have to be yourself. You must act! Allow God to begin using those past experiences, and then *combine* them with your gifts and talents! This is how you'll tap into your calling, which in turn, will result in you living out your God-given destiny!

SILENCING THE CRITICS, BUT STILL LISTENING

As you begin to act on your gifts and calling, you will start to bring some attention to yourself. The devil and his demons are *not* going to leave you alone just because you've decided to let Christ live through you. In fact, just the opposite happens—reinforcements get sent in. What happens next is this: YOU WILL COME UNDER ATTACK…so prepare yourself. Lots of people, both Christian and non-Christian, will begin to hate you on a level unlike you've ever known before. So always keep in mind what Jesus said, "If the world hates you, remember that it hated me first" (see John 15:18).

As you move forward in *consistent* action, y you will even begin to wonder, *"What is going on here? Why is this happening to me?"* My friend, this is part of it, so don't get discouraged. You will begin to catch flack from both the religious people *and* from the non-believers, but it doesn't end there. Close family members and friends won't quite get this either at first, mainly because this *outward* version of you is brand new to those *around* you. They don't know who this person really is just yet, so give it time. God is giving you a new reputation, one that matches up with your insides. Everything is going to be okay—eventually. Remember that God *strengthens* us through people testing our faith. It's a good thing! (See James 1:3).

Frankly, they just aren't used to this new version of you for one of two reasons:

1. **You are an old Christian who is finally acting like your true self**. You've been saved a long time, but you've decided to stop suppressing your perfect spiritual self—so they don't recognize you.

2. **You are a new Christian who has new desires**. You recently got saved, therefore your new, heavenly spirit is protruding out of you through your actions and attitudes—and they just ain't used to that.

So just let things play out while staying focused on Jesus! Begin to rest in His grace each day as you get to know Him more and more, and most of all, enjoy your life! No matter *who* begins to come against you—ENJOY YOUR LIFE! In the midst of any kind of struggle, again, ENJOY YOUR LIFE! Christ is *with* you while everything is being re-formed and re-shaped all around you! Your relationships will change, your influence will change, and your *critics* will change. Your critics will not only change, but they will come flooding out from the woodwork like cockroaches. Who cares. Ignore them. Most of your critics are just jealous, so don't worry about that.

"MOST OF YOUR CRITICS ARE JUST JEALOUS, SO DON'T WORRY ABOUT THAT."

When you come under attack, at first, you will question yourself greatly and try to appease everyone—I know this all too well. Let me save you some time: *you can't please everyone, so don't ruin your life trying to.* I struggled tremendously with this in the beginning of acting on my calling all because I wanted everyone to like me—which is impossible. God has taught me that when others try to discourage me, that's originating from the devil, plain and simple. Satan is our accuser so he will attempt to discourage us by way of the words and actions of others (see Revelation 12:10).

No, I'm not saying that *they* are the devil, I'm saying that our enemy works *through* people—both Christians and non-Christians—by influencing their minds. The good news is that God knows what your goals are, even when you fail! He sees your effort in action! So even if you haven't been a Christian for very long, or even if you don't know tons of Scripture—FIRE AWAY! God uses new believers just as much as He uses someone who's been acting on their calling for 60 years! DON'T BE AFRAID! Like a proud father with his energetic toddler, God will clean up your messes when you mess up. It's okay. Keep going.

The Holy Spirit will begin to teach you what you should and *shouldn't* be paying attention to. He will bring in mentors to help you, and He will remove bad influences as well. So when someone is extremely harsh and critical of you—rather than lovingly directing you—shrug it off. MOVE FORWARD. Don't worry about trying to make everyone happy with you! YOU CAN'T! Instead, keep *your style* and *your voice* the same. Allow yourself to learn from others while keeping your focus on Jesus. He will always direct you in the right way.

Be sure to remember the good things *He* says about you, and forget about the bad things that others say. After all, they don't define you and He does! This is why you should never find your identity in the approval of *people*. But I do need to say you should always consider—even if it's a very small amount—that what your critics are saying might have *some* credence. Keep it in the proper perspective, but still consider it. Criticism from anyone should immediately be brought to God and asked about, "Is there something important in what they are saying? What do *you* think?" And if God says, "Yes, this needs to be adjusted," then do it. This is how we stay humble and constantly grow in Christ. Being corrected based on the truth of God's Word is a very good thing and it ultimately leads to wisdom.

—⊗⊗⊗—

"DON'T WORRY ABOUT TRYING TO MAKE EVERYONE HAPPY WITH YOU! YOU CAN'T!"

—⊗⊗⊗—

However, if God says, "Ignore that," then look at their criticism as of no importance, no matter who they are. Listen to them as you would a barking dog behind a fence—it's just noise. It's harmless and it means nothing. Let them bark until their heads fall off, smile, mind your own business, and keep walking. Respect the opinion of *everyone* but never live by anyone's opinion of you. If you do, then you will be a very miserable person. Peoples' opinions change daily, God's never does! So stay centered on what *He* says about you! After all, He lives inside you and He knows you the best.

PAIN AND ROOTS

Whether it comes from understanding how to handle critical people, or from trying to allow yourself to rest in God's grace instead of your own works, the pain we encounter while growing in Christ is extremely important for our well-being. Here's why:

> The pain that our unrenewed mindsets experience while first allowing Jesus to live through us is what causes His supernatural roots to grow deeper into our thinking.

Don't confuse your mind with your spirit. By grace through faith your spirit is perfect, complete, and brand new. It's woven together with Christ like wicker. But your mind is different—it grows. Let's get the description of your flesh out of the way real quick. Your flesh is but a tool for your spirit to use while in this physical realm—there isn't anything wrong with your flesh. It is holy and blameless just like your spirit and soul is (see 1 Thessalonians 5:23). However, your flesh has a supernatural parasite in it which will never go away as long as your flesh lives. This parasite is called *sin* (see Romans 7:23, Genesis 4:7). Just like gravity impacts your flesh into staying glued to this planet, sin impacts your body and mind's desires, even when you get your new spirit. This is why it's such a battle when you first become a Christian, your mind is being renewed to your righteousness and your body is learning new, holy habits. (See Romans 7, Galatians 5).

Pain will come to your unrenewed mindsets as you get to know who you really are in Christ. Why? Because you aren't used to thinking this way, even though it's authentic. We are 100% holy but our thoughts mature to our holiness—we are not our thoughts. Our actions and attitudes grow to match up with our spirit. Old thinking can be animalistic but *you* control yourself by simply being your *true* self. The pain you experience as you grow in the grace of God is coming from *allowing* Him to reshape your thought life (see Philippians 1:6, 4:8, Romans 12:2).

Just because you're a Christian that doesn't necessarily mean you are *enjoying* an intimate relationship with Jesus. True intimacy with Him begins when you understand His love, *but* you won't begin to understand His love without experiencing the pain He felt—both for you *and* for others. Feelings happen in your *soul*.

For example, each time I see Mel Gibson's *The Passion of the Christ*, it's hard for me to *not* weep. The first time I saw it, I walked out of the movie theatre still sobbing. I finally understood the pain Jesus went through to save me. It was *pain* that solidified His love for us! So we should look to that example in our relationships with others! It wasn't through an easy way out or a nice, comfy, powerful earthly throne—it was through torture. Understanding His pain is what embeds His roots into our thinking. In order for us to grow in the knowledge of His unconditional love, we have to express Him. As we do, we begin to understand our own value to God, but also the value of everyone else.

When I first understood this, a new eruption of wanting to get this news out there for everyone else to know about, immediately consumed me. In the beginning, I was simply regurgitating everything I was learning. My roots weren't very deep just yet, so instead, I was living off the high. This resulted in me becoming an out-of-control firehose of Christianity. I was still getting my energy from my emotions, rather than from my identity. My actions and attitudes became extremely aggressive and sometimes disrespectful and unloving as I constantly had to seek out *better* feelings.

What I didn't understand was that my mind was being transformed and my immature methods of coping were being put under control as God taught me to *not* live by how I feel.

I was studying Christ heavily, daily, and spouting it all out while still trying to understand it and apply it to myself. I was just *so* excited, and I wanted the world to know about Jesus like I now did! But at the same time, I was still struggling with how to apply the truth of my new self to my *old* actions and attitudes. My problem was this: *I hadn't yet felt the pain that I needed to. My faith was immature, emotional, and "fluffy."* In order to establish my roots in Christ I had to go *deeper* by feeling the pain of making d different choices—choices based on my love and respect for Jesus, as well as my true identity.

"WHAT I DIDN'T UNDERSTAND WAS THAT MY MIND WAS BEING TRANSFORMED AND MY IMMATURE METHODS OF COPING WERE BEING PUT UNDER CONTROL AS GOD TAUGHT ME TO NOT LIVE BY HOW I FEEL."

As I look back on that time in my life, I believe God was very proud of this green version of me. It took a lot of courage to do what I did. For example, I was trying to let people know that forgiveness is very important to God, but I was still having a hard time with it myself. Little did I know that Jesus uses the pain from our immaturity more than anything else to establish His roots into our thinking.

"This is a process, this is a process, this is a process," I constantly said this to myself each time I messed up in order to *calm* myself. I wasn't about to give up on enjoying this new life! I still *wanted* it—I wanted to be *used* by Jesus! There was *no way* I was about to give up on my newfound drive to spread this good news! So I began to allow Jesus to dig up and break open the soil of my mind through His Word.

Of course, allowing God to activate our gifts and calling through action is exciting at first—like a honeymoon. But then the real relationship begins! The marriage! Simply dating is now over and life begins! Like a marriage, as you allow your behavior and disposition to be molded into being kind, loving, dedicated, honorable, and respectable to your spouse, you will grow deeper in love with them. The same thing happens in your relationship with Jesus, so don't be afraid of getting uncomfortable as you grow with Him.

When you begin to make positive changes in your life for Jesus, so you *can* grow with Him, you start to feel something "different" on the inside. At first you don't know what it is, but a new type of peace and confidence now rests in your soul which wasn't there before. As of now, I can personally tell you what it is, but at first I didn't know either. Further, it's not an *it* but a *who*—*the Holy Spirit!* God Himself in spirit-form dwelling *in* you and *with* you! It's amazing! You'll see what I mean soon, if you haven't just yet! It is indescribable in words, this feeling of actually having God *in* you!

YOU MUST CHOOSE IT

Unlocking your destiny comes by choice. You have to *choose* to walk by your true self each day. God is a gentleman. He *loves* you. He loves you so much that He will never force you to love Him back, and, He will never force you to act on the gifts and calling that He has placed inside of you. Yes, He'll keep talking to you about them, He'll keep saying, "Please, do *this*." But still, it's up to us to say, "Okay, Lord. I may not feel like I'm ready but I trust you. Here I am, use me." Once we finally get into agreement with God and stop listening to the lies of the devil as he tries to talk us *out* of using our gifts (he does this through the discouragement of others and by our own mistakes) *then* God can use us for great and mighty things!

Your life goes from ordinary to *extra* ordinary! This is how: *nothing and nobody can stop you once you combine your talents with Christ!* So even when a roadblock gets in your way *temporarily*—it's always for a greater good!

Those people and situations don't surprise God. He is *still* using you *and* those roadblocks at the same time!

When I finally decided to begin acting on the promptings in which the Holy Spirit was gently nudging me with, my spirit didn't want to ignore it any longer, although my old mindsets still did. We must understand that our spirit and old ways of thinking are constantly at battle with one another. Thankfully, the deeper we grow in the knowledge of our true selves and God's grace, the less likely our old thought life has any say-so in our choices.

"NOTHING AND NOBODY CAN STOP YOU ONCE YOU COMBINE YOUR TALENTS WITH CHRIST!"

When I finally decided to become vocal about my faith, I made a decision to do my very best to live out who I really was in spirit. I told myself that if I'm going to talk about Jesus all the time, then I must also live Him *out*—what a head-on collision! This was *very* difficult at first, but I made it through the hardest parts by the grace of God!

I understand that—at first—it is overly difficult to live out our perfect self, mainly because the sin of our flesh is so used to getting its way and our minds have a lot of catching up to do. Just to be real with you, to the flesh and old stinking thinking, it's like eating a basket full of sour apples. Sometimes it's pure torture but it does get easier over time.

When the flesh still ruled my choices, rather than my real self, I can remember breaking down in tears many times because I was not used to making such difficult decisions. It hurt *really* bad. But this pain taught me how to grow and mature in my faith. It taught me who I was *not*. It taught me how to trust God and not lean on my own understanding, which is what we must do to answer our calling. Any type of spiritual growth will require some fleshy and emotional pain, and if you are keeping your mind fixed on Jesus, don't forget that He was tortured.

The Bible says, "Consider it pure joy when we face trials of many kinds because we know that the testing of our faith produces perseverance, and we should let perseverance finish its work in us so that we are mature, complete, and not lacking anything" (see James 1:2-4).

MATURE! COMPLETE! NOT LACKING ANYTHING! I can't say I got those things from living by the flesh, rather than by my spirit. Matter of fact, just the opposite of all three! But this *maturity*, this *completeness*, and this *not lacking anything*, all comes from allowing Christ to finish the work in us that *He* began when we decided to let Him! WHEN WE MADE THE CHOICE TO ANSWER OUR CALLING! So answer *your* calling, today!

Part Two

YES, I BELIEVE, NOW WHAT?

Chapter 5

GOD STARTS IT, YOU LIVE
IT, HE FINISHES IT

*"And I am certain that God, who began the good work
within you, will continue His work until it is finally
finished on the day when Christ Jesus returns."*

PHILLIPIANS 1:6

GIVE YOURSELF A BREAK

So you've got some nail holes in the hands and feet of your old coping mechanisms—that's good! You're beginning to understand what Christ went through for you, and that's great! THIS IS WHERE YOUR NEW LIFE IN CHRIST GETS EVEN BETTER! You're starting to realize that you actually *did* die in spirit, and get a new spirit! Your roots are growing deeper and your spiritual maturity is blooming bigger and brighter, even to the point of God using you in a great way! Wonderful!

Keep moving forward and you will eventually go from someone who needs to be constantly coached and coddled, to *doing* the coaching and coddling yourself. Every day you'll become stronger in Christ as you get to know Him more. In order to *get* to know Him more, I've found that we should focus on a couple things:

1. Listen to Him as He speaks to your spirit.
2. Let go of yesterday and learn to forgive yourself quickly.

I've already touched on how to hear from the Spirit of God, so for this section, I'm going to focus on how to forgive yourself. If you don't learn to forgive yourself as God has forgiven you, you won't grow, but instead, you'll be a quiet Christian in the crowd with no enthusiasm. By staying focused on just how big Jesus' forgiveness is for you, it makes it easier to learn how to forgive yourself when you mess up. When we refuse to forgive ourselves—or allow ourselves to believe the lies of others *about* our forgiveness—we'll soon fall into anger, and then self-pity.

You *must* let go of yesterday! You must let go of the last hour! Don't focus on your struggles, focus on your Savior! Focus on your perfect spirit! This is imperative to growing in your relationship with Christ. Good or bad, don't focus on your *do* but instead focus on your *who*. You should never be harder on yourself than even God is, so let it go as soon as it happens. Keep repenting of the stuff you know God wants you to repent of, keep bringing your struggles and set-backs to Him in prayer, and be easy on yourself. Learn from it and move forward—no matter how long it takes. Always remember that living out your spiritual perfection is a process, and this process will not end on this side of heaven (see Philippians 1:6).

"KEEP REPENTING OF THE STUFF YOU KNOW GOD WANTS YOU TO REPENT OF, KEEP BRINGING YOUR STRUGGLES AND SET-BACKS TO CHRIST IN PRAYER, AND BE EASY ON YOURSELF."

If you don't let go of the past each day, the devil will convince you that you are no good to God or that you're a victim—THESE ARE LIES. Eventually, you'll slip into severe frustration and allow yourself to be mistreated by others because you still don't understand how valuable you are to God. You will never enjoy living the life Jesus died to give you by focusing on people's guilt and shame. So forgive yourself every day and advance ahead in His grace!

By doing this you will also set a great example for others to see. People will start to notice that just because you messed up that doesn't mean you *give* up. Also, they'll notice that you never complain. Nobody likes a whiny Christian; whiny Christians can be more annoying than arrogant Christians because there is always *something* wrong happening or *someone* to moan about. They can be very emotionally draining, so keep your attitude positive.

Christians shouldn't *be* whiney anyway! We shouldn't constantly be verbalizing our worries or always down-in-the-mouth, struggling for answers—NO! WE ARE STRONG IN CHRIST! Even when we are weak, we are *still* strong (see 2 Corinthians 12:10). If we have a bad day, we regroup, stand up, and march forward knowing *who* is our leader! We keep our confidence and trust in Him! *This* is what God wants from us! This is how we show people who Jesus really is! He's not a sour-puss! He is confident and content, and He lives *in* us!

"GODLINESS IS SIMPLY BEING OURSELVES AS CHILDREN OF GOD, CONTENTMENT IS CHOOSING TO ENJOY IT."

Contentment means we are completely satisfied with where we're currently at, while always holding out hope for growth and improvement. Contentment allows us to choose to enjoy life based on knowing who we are in Christ. Joy is a fruit of the Spirit who lives in us (see Galatians 5:22-23). Nobody can stop us from having joy because it comes from within. Contentment comes from resting in God's grace (see Hebrews 4:11). The Bible says, "Godliness with contentment is of great gain" (1 Timothy 6:6).

Godliness *and* contentment. Godliness is simply being ourselves as children of God, contentment is choosing to enjoy it.

This is a journey. We can't complete a journey as long as we are standing still, so keep taking steps day by day to enjoy this journey the most. As we make headway in this journey, God prepares us for an eternal glory in heaven with Him which will last forever. So when you mess up, know that He's not mad at you, but instead, *committed* to you (see 2 Timothy 2:13). God is the only *true* Promise Keeper, and we are the ones who enjoy that promise (see Hebrews 6:13). As long as you have this flesh, which is infected with sin, you will make mistakes. But the Father will never give up on you because Jesus will never die again *and* because you have a new spirit which is co-mingled with His (see Hebrews 7:25, Romans 6:6, Colossians 3:3).

However, over time your life will begin to look different. The heavenly trajectory of your actions and attitudes *will* keep moving upward! In other words, you will mature in Christ as time goes on (see 1 Corinthians 13:11, Philippians 3:14). So rather than being hard on yourself, or constantly "trying really hard to be good," stop that. Be nice to you! Don't make me come over there! Life is so much more fun and enjoyable by you just being easy on you!

"But Matt, what if I'm too easy on myself and I keep making bad choices?"

Friend, trust God's grace. Trust *yourself*. God's grace actually works wonders in helping us make proper choices. The same very grace which saved you will also mature you (see Titus 2:11-12). Show *yourself* some grace and you'll see! God will let you know if something is not okay, don't worry about that or stress out looking for it—you'll know. His Spirit will guide your spirit all day long (see Romans 8:16). So just be yourself, *forgive* yourself, and enjoy God's grace.

SELF SACRIFICE OR CHANGE OF CLOTHES?
Christ indwells us and we have a heaven-ready spirit, so we will have a natural bend toward sacrificing certain things in our lives which no longer matches up with us. We don't sacrifice stuff and make changes in order to

earn anything, or to make sure we don't lose anything, but instead to simply shake off the grave clothes. Like Lazarus stumbling out of the tomb after being dead for days, Jesus told him, "Take off your grave clothes" (see John 11:44). When we start to walk in the manner of who we are inside, self-sacrifice is not even a real thing. Instead, we are just being ourselves by not making sinful choices. Sinful choices will *never* fit us—they will be uncomfortable.

As Christians, sin will never match up with us because we've been born of God. John said we can't even go on sinning because God's seed is in us—as in, our *spirits* don't even have the ability to sin (see 1 John 3:9). So self sacrifice is another way of saying the *flesh's* sacrifice, or *mind-renewal* sacrifice. I mean, what are we really agreeing to when we choose to not sin? Being ourselves? The word sacrifice is thrown around in Christians circles quite often, but we aren't really sacrificing anything when we are simply doing what we know we *should* be doing: being who we are.

Learning this fact about our spiritual DNA also keeps us from becoming door-mats who get stomped on because of some stupid religious rule of submission. Again, what are we submitting to? Once we truly know who we are, we will develop the correct attitude of, "No, you're not going to treat me like a dog, because I'm not a dog. I have heavenly blood in my veins and I deserve to be treated with respect."

Ripping off your grave clothes gives you *extreme* confidence and breathing room! Understanding who you are as God's child allows you to be able to stand up to people—in the right way! So tear those dingy clothes off and holler like Tarzan!

LET JESUS USE YOUR PAST

Jesus didn't give you a perfectly clean spirit just so you can say you never had a dirty one. Instead, He wants to *use* the testimony of the old you *for* your purpose. He wants to use your old mess for a brand new message! So share! You've got nothing to be ashamed of any longer! Your past is dead, so carry it with you and show it off to others like the hide of a beast you've slain. Walk around confident and proud, saying, "Hey guys, check this out! Jesus helped me kill this thing, and He will do the same for you!"

I highly recommend that you get your past out into the open and then let the chips fall where they may. It is *such* a relief when you do this, and afterwards, you have nothing to fear any longer because it's *right* there for everyone to see. What else can happen? It can't be shoved in your face anymore, and the devil can't shamefully use it against you. You've nailed it to the Cross by handing it over to Jesus through your spiritual death and resurrection. So share your testimony and He will take it from there!

LET YOUR LIGHT SHINE FOR ALL TO SEE!

More than anything else this world needs to get to know Jesus. As Christians, we are supposed to *show* the world who He really is by being *who* He has made us to be. In the midst of darkness we should be shining our light brightly for all to see, but doing so in such a manner that Christ becomes attractive. Christ *is* attractive, He's not forceful! Did Jesus force Himself onto you? No, He didn't. Instead, He shared His truth with love, and then He let you make your own choice as to whether or not you'd believe. We should do the same.

So many Christians get upset about *others* not believing, and I get it. I know that those who reject God's Spirit will not inherit His Kingdom. However, we shouldn't allow the choices of others to destroy our own enjoyment of Christ. There is a quasi-Christian mantra going around of, "I gotta stand in the gap for them!" and truth be told, *we* can't stand in the gap for anyone when it comes to their salvation (see 1 John 5:16). We can pray for them diligently, we can share, and we can show love, but at the end of the day, if we are allowing the fear of someone else's salvation to cause us anxiety, that is no way to live—and that is not coming from God.

This type of mindset is a form of *Christian codependency* and it's not healthy for our soul. Sure, Jesus wants everyone to believe but this is *still* a personal choice that each created being must make on their own. So if we aren't enjoying our relationship with God because someone else refuses to believe, then our own light will be covered up until we stop this madness. And if we try to force people to believe, we will live frustrated, depressed, and angry—because we don't have this ability. So give people room to breathe, relax, and just be yourself: a light (see Matthew 5:14).

Let me ask you a question. If you are standing in a room and someone flips the lights off, what's the first thing you say? More than likely it will be, "Who turned off the light?" You'll never say, "Who turned *on* the darkness," because you already know that someone turned *off* the light. This proves that we naturally know that darkness cannot overcome light—it's impossible. All darkness really is, is the *absence* of light. So this teaches us that in order to get light back into a dark world, we need to shine bright! We need to be ourselves!

A quick tip on how to do this is to ignore the discouragement of the devil. As I've mentioned, he will try to use both Christians and non-Christians to discourage you. He uses Christians to attempt to make you feel terrible. They will do this by trying to get you to believe you are either not doing enough, or that what you're doing is wrong. They will even strive to make you think your mistakes cause God to become so angry that He keeps taking your salvation back. These are all lies from the devil *through* Christians. Ignore it and don't let it bother you.

The enemy will also attempt to use non-Christians to discourage you. They will attack you with sarcasm and insults while trying to make you seem like a fool because you love Jesus. They *hate* your light because their hearts are dark. Most of them don't want to believe in Jesus because of their pride. Pride is why they can't wrap their minds around this wonderful good news of God's grace. They think because it's *too* simple and *too* easy, that something more is needed—or nothing at *all* is needed. Pride blinds them from believing the truth. They say they need more proof, but proof requires no faith, and faith requires no proof. Yet, they are placing their faith in more proof. It makes no sense.

"PRIDE DESTROYS FAMILIES, FRIENDSHIPS, BUSINESSES, AND COUNTRIES—NOT JUST A PERSON'S ABILITY TO BELIEVE."

They want to put the burden of proof on us, but really, it's on them. Why? Because *they* are our proof! Them being alive proves that God loves them so much that He wanted to create them! But they still want more, which equals pride. Jesus said we must "become like little children," and children are pride-free (see Matthew 18:3). They believe what is told to them without questioning it. Through this example of child-like faith, Jesus is *not* saying, "Be stupid and believe anything," instead, He's saying, "Trust me. Believe in me. I'm real." Pride keeps more people in self-bondage than anything else. Pride destroys families, friendships, businesses, and countries—not just a person's ability to believe.

Here are some final words of encouragement about what you should do with the light that is in you, the very words of Jesus Christ who *is* that light:

"You are the light of the world. A town built on a hill cannot be hidden. Neither do people light a lamp and put it under a bowl. Instead they put it on its stand, and it gives light to everyone in the house. In the same way, let your light shine before others, that they may see your good deeds and glorify your Father in heaven." (Matthew 5:14-16)

SO KEEP SHINING! Shine, shine, shine baby, shine!

Chapter 6

REPRESENT CHRIST WELL, THE WORLD IS DEPENDING ON IT

*"Everyone will know that you are my disciples,
if you have love for one another." –Jesus*

JOHN 13:35

*"We are therefore Christ's ambassadors, as though
God were making his appeal through us"*

2 CORINTHIANS 5:20

GOD'S REPRESENTATIVES AND NEW HABITS

As children of God, we have an amazing responsibility: *we are His agents! We are His ambassadors!* How awesome is that?! God uses *us* to do His bidding! He has always used people to get His message out and our generation is no different. His message of relationship and redemption through faith in Jesus Christ continues on through us. I've been saved since I was a young boy, however, around January 2011, I decided to begin allowing Christ to have His way with me. This was extremely difficult to do because the sin of my flesh and old stinking thinking ruled my life.

My lifestyle didn't match up with the character of God *or* the true character of my perfect spirit. For this reason, my life was miserable even while attaining what the world would consider "success." My everyday decisions didn't have anything to do with Jesus and this caused me tremendous suffering in my mind. I wasn't being myself, Christ's ambassador, and this denial of who I was created severe stress and anxiety. Yet, my immature mind had every excuse as to why I kept making the choices I was making.

To make matters worse, in my relationships I had countless reasons for allowing myself to be played like a puppet and treated poorly. This was primarily accomplished by others through reputation blackmail, fear, guilt, and codependent manipulation. I needed to change how I was living, as well as how I was reacting to people—that is, if I ever wanted to enjoy my real life in Christ. God wants every Christian to eventually transition from simply being born *of* God to representing Him. When we begin to do this, life becomes much more fun.

As a child of God, I'm supposed to be growing fruit of the Spirit (see Galatians 5:22-23), but by living in the manner I did, I had *no* spiritual fruit in my life. I had nothing good to show my Dad. Instead, I took advantage of my heavenly heritage and abused His grace on a daily basis. It appeared as if my life was charmed and wonderful—*online*—but in my mind my life had become pointless, meaningless, and empty. I felt like a failure because I wasn't representing my Family very well.

Since business success didn't fix my feelings of inadequacy, and since I couldn't force certain people to appreciate me, I decided to begin drinking heavily to change how I felt. This only made things worse as my poor choices began to pile up higher, the people I was trying to change got worse, and the debilitating hangovers caused my mind to drift toward the freedom of suicide. It seems weird even writing about that stage of my life, but as I've grown in my relationship with Christ, I feel sorry for that older version of me. I understand in great detail his frustrations and pain. I know all about the unfair situations he faced and the names of the people who used him. I even know about those who tried to destroy him by any means necessary. Some days, he felt so beat up and brutally betrayed, the heartache was near-crippling. Private tears and screaming was the only way to release his torture…or so it seemed at the time.

I also know about the long hours of hard work he put in—which nobody else cared about—yet, they still enjoyed the spoils as if they did all of the work themselves. I saw the sobbing on the couch and the daily fatigue because of sleepless nights—I SAW EVERYTHING! I SAW ALL OF IT! I WENT THROUGH IT WITH HIM! I WAS THERE! That was me… It was not okay how I was treated, it was painful, but God soon taught me that He uses pain to strengthen us, not defeat us.

I look back now on Old Matt, and I can honestly say that what he felt the most was loneliness. I felt all alone. Even though I was social and had many friends, my sorrow from how I was choosing to live, along with the way I was allowing people to treat me—I felt isolated. I had to change. Jesus wanted to *help* me change by teaching me that I was *never* alone. As He did, I began to feel an overwhelming prompting to begin making some serious revisions in my actions and attitudes. I also started to feel as if I was supposed to be doing something so much more with my life *for* God, than what I was currently doing—which was nothing.

This sensation increased over time and would not go away. It was like a nudge, a relentless nudge. At the time I still couldn't stand religion in general, "Those snooty church people, who needs them anyway," was how my unrenewed mind was still thinking. I only went to church once or twice a year, if that, and my prayer life was almost non-existent. Nevertheless, because of this non-stop persuasion, I finally decided to begin getting to know Jesus better. *Enjoying* my relationship with Him was my new goal in life. I had no idea this would help me represent Him so much better.

My plan was to start by reading Christian books, the four gospels of the Bible, and by way of listening to friendly Christian teachers—none of those mean, self-righteous ones. I planned on getting to know *Jesus*. Just Him. I had no desire to attend any overbearing church services where they make you feel guilty or rush you to the front as a display. I *only* wanted to understand who Jesus Christ is—not religion. In order to do this I made one very important, yet simple adjustment to my life. This new habit changed everything: I blocked off time for Jesus every single morning, no matter what, no excuses.

"I HAD NO DESIRE TO ATTEND ANY OVERBEARING CHURCH SERVICES WHERE THEY MAKE YOU FEEL GUILTY OR RUSH YOU TO THE FRONT AS A DISPLAY. I ONLY WANTED TO UNDERSTAND WHO JESUS CHRIST IS—NOT RELIGION."

This was extremely difficult to do at first because I was so tired in the morning, and I was *tired* because I usually stayed up late. So I began to go to bed a little earlier each night, just so that I could start to get up at 5 to 5:30 am. With my company taking up so much of my time, going to the gym, having hobbies, not to mention the importance of spending time with my family, I figured that getting up *early* would be the best time for me to get to know Christ without being interrupted. Plus, there is something that feels very special about getting up before the sun does and glancing out the window while sipping coffee. I love it. It is *so* peaceful. It centers me before the busyness of each day begins.

The onset of doing this was very challenging because my flesh wasn't used to it—*it* wanted to stay put in my nice, warm bed! But I was trying to form a new habit, and that habit was getting to know Jesus *for myself*. So, coffee in hand, each day I would make my way to my study and begin with just a little chat with God.

"Good morning, Lord. Thank you for another day." The first order of business was, and still is, to always thank God for what He had done for me the day before—*and* for what I knew He was currently working out but I didn't yet see any results. I then move on to talking to Him about whatever is bothering me or what I needed to change for Him but still struggling with. And then lastly, I submit my requests to Him. I always tell Him *exactly* what I would like for Him to do for me and for others. This is called *prayer*. Prayer is just talking to God, being *real* with God, and being grateful. I really had no idea how easy it was to talk to Him until I started to be myself. I prayed before, all throughout my life, but not like this. This time I felt as if I was actually starting to get to know a Person, *and I was*. Three Persons: Father, Son, and Holy Spirit—altogether, God.

In addition to prayer, I also began to make sure I read something every morning to strengthen my knowledge of His grace, something to help hone my faith and overcome my doubts. This could either be a few pages in a good Christian book, or a chapter in the Bible. I'd switch off each day, give or take, but I never missed a day of reading. I finally understood that everything in my life depended on getting to know God better. I also decided to not make a law out of reading. Whatever I decided to read, no matter how much or how little, I took all of the pressure off myself and I just read. I was not attempting to earn stuff from God *by* my reading and praying, but instead, I did so because I wanted to get to know Him more through the life of Christ. Eventually, I found myself becoming a bookworm for Jesus. If it was about Him, I wanted to read it.

SOCIAL MEDIA MINISTRY

In order to become a more vocal ambassador for Christ, I made another drastic change. For those of you who are on social media, you'll understand this all too well. As I got to know Christ more each day, I began to journal and write about it, only, I didn't just do this privately, but publicly on Facebook. Whatever I was going through in my growth with God, or learning from Jesus at that particular time, I typed it up and posted it. There was *such* a prompting in my spirit for me to do this! For some reason I *had* to write each day and post it on Facebook. At first, my old mindset fought it big time because I didn't want to lose friends or alter my reputation. I'd have my time with God, type stuff up, and then delete it before I posted it. Intimidated and afraid, I thought to myself, "There ain't no *way* I'm posting this Christian stuff, it will make people mad. And I *definitely* don't want to lose any customers who aren't Christian. Nope! I'm not do-ing it! My faith is *my* business, not anyone else's!"

However, I'd soon find out that I couldn't *not* post what I was learn-ing about, I tried! It was like trying to cork a volcano! I *had* to share this stuff about Jesus no matter what people thought! *He* wanted me to, and I couldn't fight it. The main problem with me posting about Jesus was that I said a lot of dumb stuff and misrepresented Him—*a lot*—because I was still learning. Heck, to this *day* I'm still learning. Just because my spirit was perfect that doesn't mean my theology was lined out just yet. The Spirit teaches us new stuff about Himself *over time*.

The sad thing is, during this period of grace growth and mind renewal, I hurt many people with my words and I did it quite often. I didn't mean to, but I was still trying to get my flesh under control by way of walking by my spirit. I was also attempting to lasso my wrong thought patterns. Because of my past, I was very aggressive while trying to figure out how to represent Jesus by living *out* my perfect spiritual self. To do so, I had to *unlearn* lots of bad habits and knee-jerk reactions of the flesh. Thank God for His amazing grace and unending mercy because I think about some of the stuff I said and did—and I cringe.

While growing, I caused a lot of carnage, I burned many bridges, and I unnecessarily hurt other people's feelings. The good news is, like a baby who is trying to learn how to walk, yet keeps falling over, at the inception of being who we are in Christ *outwardly*, God doesn't get frustrated or disappointed. We don't surprise Him, but instead, He is proud of us! When we fall, He doesn't yell and beat us down, He gently helps us back up each time and encourages us.

"WHEN WE FALL, HE DOESN'T YELL AND BEAT US DOWN, HE GENTLY HELPS US BACK UP EACH TIME AND ENCOURAGES US."

So even in my immature eagerness to tell others about Jesus, and fumbling all over the place, I know that I was still being used greatly by God. I now understand that *as* I messed up, I learned. The Holy Spirit was teaching me new things day by day as I scuffed up my knees quite often in the comments section of my posts—especially when dealing with aggressive unbelievers or legalistic Christians. I got to cut my teeth during many disputes and as the years have gone by, I've become a rather well-versed apologist. I'm not afraid to have any conversation with any person—Christian or not. The Holy Spirit has taught me to always be prepared to give an answer for the hope I have, but I'm supposed to do this with gentleness and respect (see 1 Peter 3:15).

Sometimes I'll go back to look at what I've written and see the growing pains in my older posts. My writings have evolved from a timid, excuse-filled, blameful, *all about me* mentality, to a loving, hopeful, *all about Christ* theology. As I sift through certain times in my life from the past, I can see clearly now that God was working hard in me, and what He was mostly working on was my trust in Him.

I actually *feel* like a good ambassador for Christ now, even when I have a tough day or difficult confrontations. All of these positive changes happened in my life because of one small new habit I formed: *daily time spent learning about Christ*. Family, friends, and co-workers all thought it was fake, or that it would be short-lived, but I knew there was no going back to living the way I was—in denial of myself. It's a wonderful feeling to know who you actually are inside, and that God is completely committed to you. It's an even better feeling to be yourself, and by doing so, help others come to know Christ.

CHURCH, BAPTISM, AND REPENTANCE

Although church attendance can be a very good thing if that church is built on God's grace, *being* a Christian is not about making a weekly trip to church. It's about *becoming* the church, an actual place where the Spirit of Christ lives and dwells with love. How often do you ask someone about

Jesus, or them being a Christian, and they immediately say, "Yeah, I go to church." Or, "Yes, I'm a Christian, but I haven't been to church in a while." Why is this? Why do so many people mentally combine their salvation with attending a building? It's because of what we've been taught, and it's incorrect. If attaining and maintaining our salvation is based on repeatedly visiting a geographical location, then we aren't really living under grace.

Growing up, I heard that if you don't go to church, you will go to hell. And if you *stopped* going to church, your punishment would be the same. Once again, these were lies the enemy placed in my mind *through people* to try to distract me from the truth that appearing at a building does not make me a Christian. Jesus died to remove the *need* for an actual building to find God, uninterrupted (see Matthew 27:51). Instead, on *this* side of the Cross, *we* are now the buildings (see 1 Corinthians 6:19). Jesus' death and resurrection also removed the need to have a priest or a "middle-man" in order to have access to God (see Hebrews 4:14-15). Through our faith in Him, we have complete admittance to the Father (see Romans 5:1-2).

So as Christ's representatives, we must make sure people know that church attendance doesn't cause us to be acceptable to God, this does: *do I believe that only Jesus can save me from my sins?* This action of belief can happen anywhere. We can become a Christian at any second of any day, at any place on earth. Although I don't recommend you going to a strip club to begin believing, but even there, you could be saved. You can *receive* your new spirit anywhere. This can happen in your car, in a jail cell, at church, in your church's parking lot, sitting at your desk at work, or at school. You can even do this on a bar stool or at the person's house you are cheating on your spouse with. Salvation is instantly free to all who believe, *not* to all who never miss a church service (see John 1:12)

If you think there's more to it then you are saying that what Jesus did on the Cross was not good enough, and that we need to add to it so that it *will* be good enough. My friend, that is incorrect. As His ambassadors, we must never live by a legalistic mindset. For those who *do* choose to live legalistically, they will rebuttal my statements with, "No, salvation by grace through faith is *not* good enough because of two things: baptism and repentance. The Bible says we need both."

I agree. We need both. But we need to *define* both. First, for baptism. The word *baptism* simply means "placed into" or "placed inside of." When we are baptized *into* Christ, our spirits are literally being place inside of Him (see Colossians 3:3). If you read the sixth chapter of Romans, Paul refers to our need for baptism, but not one time does he mention water. This is because Paul knew that no amount of water in all the universe could possibly wash away our sins (see 1 Corinthians 1:14-17). Further, anything we *do* or *don't do* in order to *get* our salvation is not authentic because it nullifies grace. Paul made this clear to the Romans in chapter 11 of his letter, "And if by grace, then it cannot be based on works; if it were, grace would no longer be grace" (Romans 11:6).

Someone might fire back at me with, "Water baptism is not a work!" but I'd have to say that is wrong. A "work" is anything *we* do or don't do in regard to our attitudes or actions to achieve something. This is why the word *grace* means "undeserved." Anything we work for, we earn. If we are attempting to get salvation by placing our physical bodies into a liquid, that's a *work* of ours. So yes, baptism is important and necessary to be saved, but it has nothing to do with water. Water baptism is simply a celebration of our *spiritual* birthday! It's *not* the actual moment we become spiritually reborn! *That* moment is finalized when our spirit is placed into Christ, by grace through faith. Should we get water baptized? Absolutely! Refusing to do this would be the same as refusing to celebrate your birthday—it's important because *you* are important!

"WATER BAPTISM IS SIMPLY A CELEBRATION OF OUR SPIRITUAL BIRTHDAY! IT'S NOT THE ACTUAL MOMENT WE BECOME SPIRITUALLY REBORN!"

Next, let's talk about repentance. Until I truly understood grace, this was a fighting word. Legalistic preachers kept me in constant fear of hell because of my "refusal to truly repent of all my sins." This is a misleading *trick* statement because we don't repent of all of our incorrect actions and attitudes to *get* saved in the first place. Instead, we repent of our unbelief in Christ as our Savior. Along with baptism into God's Spirit, repentance of unbelief in Jesus is all that is required to be saved—and *both* happen at the same time!

The book of Hebrews is a wonderful example of just how important repentance of unbelief in Jesus is. This letter was primarily written to the unbelieving Jews, the ones who had heard about the Messiah from the best gospel teachers, but yet, still refused to believe. This is why the author writes, "If we deliberately keep on sinning after we have received the knowledge of the truth, no sacrifice for sins is left, but only a fearful expectation of judgment and of raging fire that will consume the enemies of God" (Hebrews 10:26-27).

The key words to notice here are, "no sacrifice for sins is left," as in, the blood of bulls and goats, which is what the Jews used for their sacrifices to God *for* their sins (see Hebrews 9:22). The author was saying, "You've heard about Jesus' final sacrifice for sin, but you still keep bringing animal blood to the temple to be forgiven. That blood means nothing now, only Jesus' does. Believe in *His* blood, and be saved."

For centuries, Hebrews 10:26 and 27 have been taken out of context by people who don't understand the gospel. They've done this in order to create fear in the minds of Christians so that they'll shape up—but this is not *how* God wants us to shape up. This passage wasn't even written *to* believers but to the unbelieving Hebrews. For proof of this, all you have to do is read up *to* this verse, chapters one through ten, as well as the following verse, which refers to the Law of Moses, which *they* were trying to stick with.

"So Matt, you're saying that behavior repentance doesn't matter?" No, that's *not* what I'm saying at all. Of course behavior repentance matters. Not only does behavior repentance matter, but so does *attitude* repentance.

Why do they matter? Because people are watching us! We are Christ's ambassadors! (See 2 Corinthians 5:20).

Repentance simply means "turn from," and as we grow in the knowledge of who we really are in spirit, we will organically turn from the sin that our old mindsets want to keep. But make no mistake, turning from *any* incorrect attitude or action doesn't save us or keep us saved, *only* turning from *not* believing in Jesus d does. Trying to keep track of repenting of everything wrong we do and say is exactly what the enemy wants us to do. He wants us to be uber-legalistic. So instead of giving that nincompoop his way, we should focus on walking by who we really are, and *then* we will be sure to represent God in the proper manner!

Chapter 7

FIGHT BACK!

*"But we are not of those who shrink back and are destroyed,
but of those who have faith and preserve their souls."*

HEBREWS 10:39

"Do not be overcome by evil, but overcome evil with good."

ROMANS 12:21

*"Put on the full armor of God, so that you can
take your stand against the devil's schemes."*

EPHESIANS 6:11

EVIL EXISTS, FOR NOW

Evil *does* exist. It exists simply because God did not make robots. Creating us in His own image, He wanted to be sure we can make our own choices like He does. So, He gave us *free will*. Free will is a double-edged sword because it allows us the ability to make good choices *or* evil choices. *We* choose. God doesn't choose *for* us. Yes, He has a good plan for our lives, but it's still up to us to step *into* that plan by accepting Christ as our Savior and then *acting on* our calling. It's ready, waiting, and available—and it has been since before time (see Psalm 139:16)—but even though His plan for us is on a platter, we still have to decide on our own if we will receive it, and then walk it out. We don't *have* to do this, and He won't force us, He loves us too much. Your God-given destiny is always at hand, but you still have to *choose* it. When we do so, we begin to *fight* evil, rather than contribute to its cause.

Make no mistake, God *is* good. He doesn't even have the ability to *be* evil—evil can't be in His presence. This is part of the reason why heaven is so wonderful, because of the complete absence of evil. God is also all-loving. I've quoted this verse several times in this book, but let me reiterate: God *is* love (see 1 John 4:8). Love is not just a characteristic of His, but *what* He is.

On the other hand, there is also an evil force in this world. Evil is ready and available for us to choose because without it we could not *choose* to love God or *choose* to make good choices that match up with our spiritual perfection. Without the option of evil, we would be puppets; walking, talking, aimless bags of meat with pointless lives. God would be directing us like army figurines and no choices would be necessary. This is why without being able to choose good *or* evil, we wouldn't truly be alive. We *need* free will to have life!

Without free will, all of us would simply be entertainment for a cruel God. Like foosball players in His heavenly game-room, we'd stand stiff, waiting for the next ball to drop so that we can be spun by Him. No control. No meaning. No choices. No life. So without the option of evil, free will would be completely removed, therefore canceling out our "image of God" abilities. This ultimately proves that it is *us* who chooses to make good or bad decisions—God doesn't do this for us. The bad decisions we choose to act on are also known as *sin*.

"WITHOUT FREE WILL, ALL OF US WOULD SIMPLY BE ENTERTAINMENT FOR A CRUEL GOD. LIKE FOOSBALL PLAYERS IN HIS HEAVENLY GAME-ROOM, WE'D STAND STIFF, WAITING FOR THE NEXT BALL TO DROP SO THAT WE CAN BE SPUN BY HIM."

God wants us to know that the evil in this world is not directed by Him, but instead by a parasite in our flesh called sin and by a being named *Satan*. I went over the parasite of sin in a previous chapter, so let's focus on how Satan influences us to *choose* to *act on* sin. Satan is not omnipresent like God. He is a fallen angel just like any other demon, only he is their leader. Since he can't be everywhere at once, he has countless amounts of evil workers called *demons* who represent h his diabolical nature.

God only allows their existence and influence for one reason: *for us to have an option*. Remember, we have to have more than one option in order to express our free will. Just like God loves you very much, Satan hates you very much! He hates *anything* good in your life, and he will do his very best to obliterate it, so let's make something perfectly clear: *the devil is the root-cause of all death and destruction on this planet*. When he tempted Eve and she *chose* to sin, the world instantly became non-holy and sin entered into the world—it wasn't here before that (see Genesis 3:14-19, Romans 5:12). This is why we must always keep in mind that anything *good* comes from our loving God, and anything *bad*, or evil, comes from our main enemy and this fallen planet which *he* caused to fall *through* our sin.

Both God and Satan are fighting for each human being's spirit. Like God, *we* are spirits, everlasting. Our spirits will never just "go away." Our *flesh* is temporary, but our spirits will last forever. We *will* live on, with or without God, and right now, since we are still in this flesh, God allows us to choose. This short life is but a prequel to our permeant lives. For this reason, we must be reborn *of* God *in* spirit (see John 3:3, Romans 6:6). All of us have the God-given right to choose to do this, or not, through believing in Christ as our Savior. He wants us to decide *on our own* to love Him and accept our adoption into His family through Jesus (see John 3:16, Ephesians 1:5).

Satan wants to make sure this does not happen. The Bible says in Ephesians 6:12, "Our our struggle is not against flesh and blood, but against the rulers, against the authorities, against the powers of this dark world and against the spiritual forces of evil in the heavenly realms." There is a battle going on right now! It is *us* who ultimately tips the scales *through* our free will as to which side we're on! WE CHOOSE! God and Satan do not choose for us! Once we choose to join God's Family through faith in Christ, we get victory over sin *and* the enemy while still here on this planet! (See 1 Corinthians 15:57).

FIGHT BACK BY OVERCOMING ADDICTIONS

Another wonderful way you can begin to fight the evil which is so prevalent in this world, is by letting God teach you that you weren't meant to be addicted to anything—or anyone. Not only does He want you to break free from your addictions, afterwards, He wants you to use your testimony to help others who are still struggling with the same things (see Revelation 12:10). Addictions are the byproducts of slowly believing the lies of the enemy. He wants you to *think* you gotta have it, but in reality you don't. As a child of God, you have everything you possibly *need* right now at this very moment because of Christ living in you! (See Ephesians 1:3).

Although we have all we need in our spirit, by acting on certain addictions, over time, our *bodies* begin to *physically* need it. As a result of our flesh's cravings—not us, but the flesh (see Romans 8:9)—all hell breaks loose around us when it doesn't get what it craves. When we've gone this deep into our addictions, sometimes extra steps are needed through the medical field to help flush out the physical issues we may have and can no longer ignore.

This is no joke and why we need Christ's help to set us free. Once we realize that we weren't created to be addicted to anything but a relationship with God, we also find out that our true spiritual selves aren't slaves to any substance, sex, food, thrill, or whatever. We are *not* slaves, and that's what addictions make us out to be (see John 8:34, Galatians 4:7, Romans 8:15). We aren't slaves to booze, to orgasms, to drugs, to pizza, to money, to religion, to public approval, to golf, to exercise, or to video games—WE ARE NOT SLAVES—we are free people in Christ! (See John 8:36).

Satan starts in on us from the time we are conceived, trying to kill us and ruin our lives in whatever way possible. The temptation of addictions are one of his best weapons against us, one of his nuclear bombs. Like Hiroshima and Nagasaki, *complete devastation* is what ensues after an addiction takes hold of our mind. So we, as Christians, must not stick our heads in the sand any longer about such a taboo subject. We have *got* to talk about it! We have got to stop alienating people who are struggling with addictions, and instead, reach out to them with non-judgmental, unconditional love.

—◈◈◈—

"ADDICTIONS ARE ONE OF HIS BEST WEAPONS AGAINST US, ONE OF HIS NUCLEAR BOMBS."

—◈◈◈—

When we shun those who have addictions, or worse, religiously look down on them, the devil then compounds the darkness they are fighting through *our* shame, guilt, and self-righteous condemnation. By saying such things as, "A good Christian would never get drunk or high all the time," or, "No godly man or woman would *ever* succumb to porn," these two phrases cause even *more* damage. As a person who is in recovery for alcoholism, those are some of the worst things you could ever say to an addict because it takes *no* pressure off of them, and places *no* emphasis on our identity in Christ.

"JESUS NEVER USES GUILT TO MAKE US WANT TO CHANGE. INSTEAD, HE USES LOVING CONVICTION."

The bottom line is, we were made for more! Addictions hold us back! This is why Jesus never uses guilt to help us make healthy changes, instead, He lets us know we can eat at His table no matter what. Why does He speak the truth about our perfect spirits to even someone who is acting on an addiction? BECAUSE HE KNOWS WE ARE HOLY SAINTS! (See Colossians 1:22, Hebrews 10:10, Romans 6:6). Christ says, "That's not you. I *know* you. Come, let's talk." He shows us grace and who we truly are *in* Him. This is what ultimately brings about change: *the truth of our identity.* Guilt and shame are just more weapons used by Satan to keep us in bondage because it makes us think that our efforts should be good enough to quit on our own.

For me, I've struggled with many addictions but alcoholism is what I talk about the most. There are countless amounts of closet alcoholics in this world—and even more in denial—and my desire is to teach them about the freedom found in walking *out* their spiritual perfection in Christ.

From the age of 15, all the way up until I got sober at 32 years old, I drank too much, too often. Alcohol consumption was a major problem for me. Then, on May 8th, 2014, Jesus Christ began to set me free from this bad habit as we worked together. In an effort to help others battling the same thing, I shared my story on Facebook for all the world to see. Once sober, the enjoyment of my relationship with Jesus expanded to stratospheric levels. Here's the post:

I'm in recovery for alcoholism, that is, the flesh's cravings and old thought processes. For years I drank way too much, way too often—even *as* a Christian. No I didn't "get all religious" to try to stop drinking, I've been a Christian since I was a kid. I just didn't start to show Jesus any real respect or love until about 2011, and little by little, by allowing Him to renew my mind, He's molded me into who I am today.

However, I *was* religious *while* drinking. Heck, I would testify with a beer in my hand, drunk as a skunk! The whole time not thinking there was anything wrong with such behavior. And really, there's nothing *wrong* with alcohol in itself, it's just a liquid. Even Jesus enjoyed wine. If you look at His first recorded miracle in John 2, that wasn't grape juice He created. It was the best wine the people had ever tasted!

The grace-confused Christians want you to think that alcohol *was*n't fermented in the Bible. This is silly. Even Paul said, "Don't get drunk on wine because it leads to debauchery" (see Ephesians 5:18). You can't get drunk on grape juice. People drank wine back then like we drink water or soda today, they had it with nearly every meal. Water wasn't readily available or always clean to drink, wine was. So when Paul advised the church in Ephesus to not get drunk, it was because he knew what drunkenness *leads* to: debauchery. What is debauchery? It's bad, stupid, immoral, regrettable stuff. It's what you do and how you act when you get smashed.

Although there's nothing wrong with alcohol, there *is* something wrong with *me* drinking it. I can't. I don't have an off-button. I crave more and more!

However, if a person doesn't have a problem with alcohol—and this is a big *if*—go ahead and have a drink or two. It's not a sin to drink, it's a sin to get drunk. It's a sin to do moronic crap *while* drunk. If you have to constantly ask yourself, "Do I have a problem?" then more than likely you do.

Some people can have a little wine or *one* margarita and be done. They won't even think about it anymore. Me? Ha! It's like lighting a powder keg! "We going down tonight!" I want to polish off that bottle of wine! I'll have the entire Margarita pitcher and shots! Oh, and some beers too!

Now I can *try* to fight it, but I'd be fooling myself. The addiction of my unrenewed thinking wants more. It's not *me*, me—the real me. I'm a perfect, holy spirit (see Colossians 1:22, 2 Corinthians 5:17). It's the urges of my off-kilter thoughts. I want to be clear about that.

I want to make sure you understand that as saints—as Christians—we are spirits who have souls and we live in a body. We are heaven-ready this very moment but our minds are constantly changing depending on whether or not we're expressing our true nature. Our physical bodies are innocent too. They are shells *for* our spirit. There's nothing wrong with our bodies whatsoever. They have cravings and impulsive desires which are activated by their five senses.

My taste buds enjoy the flavor of alcohol. My physical brain enjoys the euphoria of a buzz. These things aren't sinful but can become something I *allow* to be sinful when I obsess over them. Even my hands enjoyed the touch of a cold bottle of beer and my lips did too, but my body is not sinful. It's a tool for my spirit to use in this temporary physical realm.

Understanding this separation is *so* important because you will be able to divorce your *who* from your *do*. This distinction will help anyone recover from any addiction, not just booze. Christian, you are *not* what you do—good, bad, or indifferent. You are who you are by your supernatural rebirth into the family of God.

So when I controlled my drinking, I couldn't enjoy it; and when I enjoyed my drinking, I couldn't control it. Once I started, I was off to the races! I'm either going to drink a ridiculous amount and then binge-eat and pass out, or, I'll be grumpy and extremely agitated if I couldn't get access to more!

I liked to drink because it relaxed me…"Ahhhhhhh…" (Again, remember this is not the real me. This is how I thought and felt). There was nothing quite like that first beer and shot, but then *after* I was nice and relaxed, I'd become overly excited! I'd become the smartest man alive with "Great business ideas!" I look back now at Old Matt—the version of me who hadn't yet allowed God to begin renewing his mind—and I want to grab him, hug him, and say, "Hey, you weren't made for this. You were made for so much more."

I was only fooling one person and that was myself. Unbeknownst to me, at that time in my life I was being a puppet for the devil. Not that he was in me, that's impossible. Satan can't even touch believers (see 1 John 5:18). But I didn't recognize his voice. Therefore, my choices were selfish and arrogant. I refused to take responsibility for the damage I was causing. This happens to countless people as their lives unnecessarily fall apart. They get advice from friends and family who can't even manage their own lives. These people dole out terrible counsel, never saying, "You need to pray about this. God will lead you in the right direction if you'll listen to Him."

But problem drinkers drink for one main reason. If someone says otherwise, they're lying to you because they're stuck in denial. Here it is: *We want to feel different.* That's it. If we are sad, we want to feel happy. If we are stressed, we want to feel relaxed. If we are uncomfortable, we want to feel comfortable. If we feel like a failure, we want to feel like a winner. If we are bored, we want to feel entertained. Truth be told, if we are *already* extremely excited and happy, we want to feel even *more* excited and happy! We want to keep our buzz going strong! Why do you think we stay sloshed until the wee hours of the morning?

We're not trying to hurt people, we just want to *feel* different. Most people who struggle with alcoholism are extremely caring and sensitive; two very reasons why we drink. Being extremely caring and sensitive can lead to accepting unacceptable behavior from others on a grand scale. It can lead to enabling and people-pleasing, which always leaves us hurt.

Our way of thinking is off. If we can get our thoughts lined up with the truth of God, sobriety will happen organically. However, when we stay in our addiction it's because the enemy has convinced us of a huge lie: "You will only like yourself by getting away from who you think you really are!"

What a liar! We are God's children! We are set apart and seated in the heavenly realms! We've been blessed with every spiritual blessing! We are God's masterpieces! (See John 1:12, 1 John 3:1, Ephesians 1:3, 2:6,10).

But yet, if we don't *know* these truths about who we really are, Satan easily festers fear in our minds. He confuses us. This mental instigator heaps mounds of condemnation and low self-worth into our thought processes with each sip we take. "Just look at you. You are only likable when you have a buzz. You can't do anything without alcohol. You can't even function! If only you could stay drunk permanently, then you'd finally be yourself!"

What a *freaking* liar.

Friend, ignore that garbage and stay focused on the truth! How do you know the truth! God's Spirit in you *teaches* you the truth! (See John 14:26, 2 Corinthians 3:8). He teaches you who you really are, sober! You are very special, sober! Even *more* special, sober! Even *more* interesting, sober! Even *more* confident, sober! Even *more* attractive, sober!

You can unlock your full potential, sober! You can reach your highest goals and achieve your dreams, sober! You can love others on the deepest level possible, sober! You can love yourself as God loves you, sober! You can forgive authentically, sober! You can live *out* who God has created y you to be in your spirit, soberrrrrrrr!

Please, believe me. You are sober. You are *not* a drunk. You are *not* addicted. You are free! (See John 8:32, Galatians 5:1).

You are God's very own child, if you believe Jesus is your Savior. If not, believe and tap into the identity God longs to give you.

So today, my friends, know this: How did I beat alcoholism? I learned who I was. That process is still ongoing, and it will not end on this side of heaven (see Philippians 1:6, Romans 12:2). In the beginning, it felt like torture. But that's only because God was reshaping my thoughts with the truth. His seed inside my soul was growing and getting stronger as it broke out of the dirt and darkness. Shooting up and out, into the light of day, I was stretching into my true self! Do you know the truth about *your* self? Christian, you are free, you *really* are. The prison door is wide open, just walk out.

OVERCOME EVIL WITH GOOD

So here we are, the home-stretch. The final sub-chapter in the final chapter of this book. Before I button this all up, I need to make a confession: I didn't think I had it in me to write any of this. I was afraid. Do you see how our old stinking thinking can sabotage God's good plans for our lives? Obviously I did have it in me because I did it! Take that, devil!

Even with the doubts in my mind, I might have come across to you as confident or well-versed, but then again, I might not have. Either way, God has taught me there's always going to be people who hate you no matter what you do. But I need to say that *any* confidence or talent I have rests completely on my bond with Christ. Yes, I've acted on my calling by completing my first book, but I didn't have to. I could have just kept this all to myself and worked on my golf swing. I could have moved along with my life and minded my own business. Even had I ignored God's promptings for me to use this gift of writing that He placed in me, I would have *still* gone to heaven, and He would *still* love me exactly the same.

My simple belief in Jesus as my Savior has already stamped my boarding pass to the afterlife with Him—and I'm enjoying that ride as we speak! Now I'm *playing* on His team: Team Jesus. After He brought me on and gave me my salvation for free, He handed me my uniform. Then He began to pump me up, "Now go. GO! Bring more to me! I'm counting on you, Matt!"

The problem is, when Christ gives us our new identity, *evil* will then attack our lives in great ways. Evil people, evil situations, and even demonic evil—EVIL WILL ATTEMPT TO STOP YOUR WORK FOR CHRIST DEAD IN ITS TRACKS! Evil will come crashing in all around you, and you will be afraid. Your confidence will sink and you will cry. On some days, you won't know what to do with the sheer amount of evil that hits you. You won't understand *why?*

When you act on your calling, evil will attempt to CRUSH your work for Christ! It will scream at you and try to make you crawl into hole and beg God to "Just take me home." So what should we do? Just *how* are we supposed to combat such evil in this world? An *atrocious* evil that is absolutely EVERYWHERE?!...

Like this.
With *one* word: good.
Good. Good. Good...Good...Good.........GOOD!
DO. GOOD.
DO GOOD!

THIS IS THE KEY TO UNLOCKING THE DEEPEST HALLWAYS IN THE MANSION OF YOUR FAITH IN CHRIST! *THIS* IS HOW YOU ENJOY HIM! Always do good! ALWAYS! You *will* win—God will win—when you do good *against* evil! When Christ finally revealed this to me *everything* changed about my faith! In turn, everything changed about my life! I went from having a mentality of being a frustrated, angry, "I gotta prove that God is right," "I gotta dislike and stay away from non-believers," "I gotta resent legalistic Christians," "I gotta retreat when I'm being mistreated"—to *then* having a mentality of love, joy, peace, and confidence! This is how you fight back and win! With goodness!

We *overcome* evil with good! Goodness stems from the love of Christ in us! Remember that we are the branches and He is the vine? Because Christ is good and our spirits are connected to Him, we too, exude goodness. He is our source! Because Christ overcame evil with good, we too, overcome evil with good! The Bible slams this home in the book of Romans, "Do not be overcome by evil, but overcome evil with good" (see Romans 12:21).

When Paul wrote this he was saying, "The best defense against Satan, is an even *better* offense through Christ." So we are to ATTACK evil *with* good, instead of attacking evil with *more* evil! When we attempt to overcome evil with evil, the devil wins in even greater ways! So we *must* remember that because of our faith in Christ, we are already on God's team! We are on His side! So don't just sit on the sidelines any longer and watch everyone else play—GET IN THE GAME! Coach Christ has already checked you in, He's looked down the bench at you, nodded His head, and said, "GET IN THERE! GO PLAY! I want you to go to work and do good things!"

"WE ARE TO ATTACK EVIL WITH GOOD, INSTEAD OF ATTACKING EVIL, WITH MORE EVIL!"

The next step is to *take* a step. But first, we gotta stand up! How? By becoming religious or aggressive? NO! God just wants you to get in the game of LIFE and play! But *how?*…With love! With *goodness*! If you will actually *do* this, then you will start to score huge numbers for Christ! You will be helping Team Jesus win more souls! *Your* contribution will help us pull ahead in the game, after that, it becomes a blowout! So we are to LOVE people! Even when hated! We are to SHOW GOODNESS *despite* evil coming up against us!

OH MY GOSH WHEN YOU DO THIS, YOU ARE *OBLITERATING* OUR COMPETITION! It's not even *close* after that! You look over to the other sideline, and coach Satan is scrambling! He's got a terrible look of distress on his face and he says, "How am I supposed to beat that?! We don't stand a chance!"

He's drawing all over his white board, trying all kinds of tactics and plays; he even sends in his toughest players, and NOTHING WORKS! NOTHING! And it's all because of *you* the superstar, who is being coached by Jesus Christ, the Superstar!

YOU ARE A *MAJOR PLAYER* IN THE GAME OF LIFE! *YOUR* LIFE, AND THE LIVES OF OTHERS! YOU ARE GREATLY IMPACTING THE TIMELINE OF HUMANITY AND ALL OF CREATION WHEN YOU ACT!

And you're doing it all for God...You're doing it in the right way, and for the right reasons. You're doing it because you love your Coach. You love your Creator. You want to make Him proud. My friend, my fellow teammate, when you get in the game and start to overcome evil with good, all discouragement gets destroyed. When you finally step into the game, you score.

You may be surprised at the ability that is in you, but *yes*, it's there. God personally placed it there. And after you finally check into the game and score, you may look down at your hand as you jog back on defense, thinking to yourself, "Whoa... How'd I do that?" But if you'll look over at Coach you'll see Him clapping loudly for you! He's bright-eyed, cheering you on and smiling *so* big! He's giddy! He's yelling out toward you, "SEE?! I TOLD YOU THAT YOU HAD IT IN YOU, KEEP GOING! C'MON!"

Because of His coaching and leadership, you decide to *stay* in the game of life and do good things! You get back on defense, and surprise even *yourself* as you TAKE the ball back, run down, and SCORE AGAIN! AND AGAIN! AND AGAAAAIN!!! AND IT'S ALL BECAUSE OF THE LOVING GOODNESS THAT IS IN YOU! YOU *CAN'T* LOSE! IT'S AN ABSOLUTE DISMANTLING OF THE OTHER TEAM!!!! EVIL IS BLOWN OUT OF THE WATER, BY *YOU*!

How is this happening?...

Because you are overcoming evil with good. You are overcoming hate with love. You are acting on your gifts and calling. And, you are personally following in the footsteps of Jesus Christ by being yourself.

Had I never checked into the game of life with Jesus leading me, had I just sat there on the bench as a weak, scared, timid Christian...had I just listened to the crowd boo and hiss at me, while the other team snickered and ran up the score...had I done that, this book would have never happened. My ministry would have never happened. My relationship with Jesus would have never been enjoyed. Instead, I would have just sat there, head hung low, afraid to play, much less contribute...but no. Jesus got up and walked toward me. He put His hands on my shoulders, knelt down, and said,

"Hey. Look at me. *Look* at me. Matthew, I have come so that you can have an abundant life. If you'll simply be yourself, you'll realize I've given you all of the power you need to be a star player for me. I'll teach you how to be an awesome fisher of men. I'll show you how to love others, like I love you. You've got it in you! It's there! I know what's in you because I placed it there. Your spirit is *good*, just like me. So never, *ever* forget, that I'm with you at all times. You are never alone. And don't you *ever* be afraid of anyone or anything. Do you hear me? Hey. Keep looking at me. Look me in the eyes...DO YOU *HEAR* ME? I'm *with* you. Always. You are going to do great things for me. I am going to do great things *through* you. I'm counting on you. Always know that I love you at all times. No matter what, nothing can change that. Now get up and get out there, and love those people! Get out there and overcome that evil with good! FIGHT BACK! FIGHT BACK! FIGHT BAAAAAAAACK!…I will be fighting with you, even until the end of time. Thank you for trusting me. Now c'mon, let's go do some wonderful, eternal things, together."

Dear friend,

Thank you so much for spending time with me through this book. I hope I was able to bring you a sense of peace and confidence in knowing more about what Christ has truly done. My prayer is for you to grow into even deeper revelations of your identity as a believer. Lastly, it would mean the world to me if you'd leave a kind review on Amazon.com, Goodreads.com, Barnes & Noble's website, or wherever you've purchased this book. Your opinion is very important and encouraging to me. I always look forward to reading reviews.

May God continue to bless you greatly, with even more knowledge, of His love for you through Jesus!

In Christ,
Matt

60 Days for Jesus, Volume 1: *Understanding Christ Better, Two Months at a Time*

"I really like Matt's writing style. He makes understanding the gospel simple and real. I have found his daily devotions to be very helpful in guiding my walk with Christ. I highly recommend his book." -*Amazon Customer*

60 Days for Jesus, Volume 2: *Understanding Christ Better, Two Months at a Time*

"This book is exactly what I needed to understand more about Jesus. I couldn't put it down. Thank you, Matt McMillen, for sharing your story to help strengthen others!" -*Amazon Customer*

60 Days for Jesus, Volume 3: *Understanding Christ Better, Two Months at a Time*

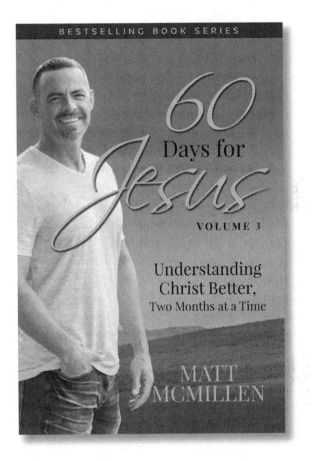

"Matt does an excellent job of providing clarity on many difficult issues every believer walks through on a daily basis. He does this by clearly articulating the scriptures to reveal the truth that really does set us free. This Volume, like the ones before, is an excellent devotional book to help any believer with their walk with God. Every page of this book is filled with the good news of God's unconditional love and grace. If you read one book this year, make it this one!" -*Amazon Customer*

The Christian Identity, Volume 1: *Discovering What Jesus Has Truly Done to Us*

"Matt brilliantly explains the supernatural transformation that happens when we become believers in the finished work of the cross. His writing style makes this easy to understand as he answers some of the toughest questions that are on so many Christians' minds today." -*Amazon Customer*

The Christian Identity, Volume 2: *Discovering What Jesus Has Truly Done to Us*

"Matt McMillen's books are amazing! You will learn so much and understand how to live your Christian life according to our Lord Jesus Christ. I've read all of his books and have shared them. I love his writing." -*Amazon Customer*

The Christian Identity, Volume 3: *Discovering What Jesus Has Truly Done to Us*

"Just as I suspected, *The Christian Identity, Volume 3*, packed as much grace and freedom punch as the first two books in this series!" *-Amazon Customer*

Made in the USA
Columbia, SC
01 March 2022

56763827R00083